FOR MOM

CONTENTS

Property for Rent – Investing in the UK

Will You Survive the Mayhem?

MARY LATHAM

ISBN-13: 978-1484855331
ISBN-10: 1484855337

BIO OF THE AUTHOR

I became a landlord in 1972, when the regulatory framework around letting was very different; to be honest, I knew next to nothing. I have spent the last forty years learning: and I continue to learn all the time.

After years of trying to talk to my local authority I founded the Association of Midlands Landlords (AML) with my landlord friend Phil Matthews in the early 90's. The Housing Department of Birmingham City Council was, at that time, managed by a 'gang' of arrogant and short sighted people who saw private landlords as the enemy, and took every opportunity to make it more difficult for us to let in the city. They also liked to boast to their colleagues, in other authorities, how they controlled private landlords in the city. At this time the idea of licensing landlords was born and Birmingham

City Council made, what was to be, their worst decision ever. They would trial landlord licensing in the city 'on a voluntary basis', simply because they had no legislation to enforce it. The normally media shy council went on national television to explain their new scheme, *Licence to Let*, and I made the mistake of taking part in that programme. The Producer had explained how he wanted to present my properties and the little effort that was needed to offer tenants safe, comfortable homes at fair rents. I am proud of the properties that I let and I was happy to take part. In the event my properties were used to castigate other landlords and to show that, while they were charging higher rents, they had not provided fire safety measures and their properties were not up to the high standards of mine. When the programme was broadcast I was horrified! They'd titled it: "Letting Them Die", and based it around the death of a young student, in a property that had no fire safety measures. It was not in Birmingham, but Stoke on Trent. My interview was edited to appear that I was criticising other landlords for the standards of their properties; in fact, nothing was further from the truth. My comments were about Birmingham City Council, constantly 'moving the goal posts', making it impossible for landlords to keep up. Far from talking about good landlords, and how the city might work with them to raise standards, the whole programme was focused on bad ones. It ended in silence, showing a series of images of people who had died in private rented property – again, none of these deaths had occurred in property within Birmingham. Any landlord watching that programme could not fail to feel ashamed of the business that they were in. I have refused many attempts to get me in front of a camera ever since and I have not shown my properties in the public arena, other than to advertise for new tenants. I understand that the media needs to attract viewers but, in my opinion, it is programmes like this that have fuelled the fear of some tenants who now need to trust private landlords to provide the homes that cannot be found elsewhere.

Our AML meetings were crowded with angry landlords and there were many suggestions about how we should fight the 'council', even to the point of hiring coaches to take us to London to petition Parliament. I am not sure how I persuaded them, but eventually the members agreed that we would simply boycott *Licence to Let*, and pass the word to other landlords to do the same, in the hope that it would die an early death. It did; council employees 'took early retirement' and 'made career changes' as a result of the costly and embarrassing failure of this high profile scheme. This taught me the power of landlords working together.

On a lighter note, it was only a few years ago that someone opened the door of the room, in the office, where the *Licence to Let* literature was stored; they had it burned – I wonder if that makes my copy a collector's item?!

This was a turning point for landlords in Birmingham, the start of a new regime, and today we probably have some of the best working relationships in the country. We now look for solutions together and, while some officers still clench their jaws when they hear the word landlord, most feel comfortable to meet us without the need to swathe the room in garlic.

Once things settled down on the 'home front', I was keen to communicate with other landlords around the country, to learn and share experiences. It was soon decided that we should join the National Federation of Residential Landlords (NFRL).

Representing the landlord members of AML, I was very privileged to meet landlords who were members of NFRL, from all over the UK. When I met Mike Stimpson, Chair of NFRL and of Southern Private Landlords, I was struck by his single minded determination to have the private rented sector (PRS) recognised as the solution to the growing housing shortage in the UK, at that time the perception of landlords was that they were the cause of housing problems. It was Mike who said, "Get landlords into associations, don't put up barriers, we can educate them once we get them in."

When I first entered the room, where over fifty

representatives of landlord associations across the UK met to discuss the business, I was awe struck. They spoke a language that I had never heard before, 'HMO's', 'PRS', 'HB', 'RSL's', 'EHO's'... I felt very out of my depth, but this wonderful group of dedicated people, mainly men, soon made me feel a part of a very important 'movement' to bring about recognition and fair play for private landlords. Before long I was invited to become a member of the National Executive of the NFRL, the first and only woman at that time; this was indeed an honour. I am sure that there were many times that they questioned the wisdom of inviting me into this group and there were many occasions when I felt the need to excuse myself, as I retreated to the ladies room to calm down and clear my head, but I would not have missed the experience of those meetings for anything. This was a huge learning curve; at that time I had only let to students, and the only knowledge I possessed of other tenant groups, was from the members of AML. These men knew so much and were generous with their knowledge and dedication. They were mostly attending these meetings at their own expense. Membership fees were used to run landlords meetings and to mail information to members (internet was still an infant). I was determined to pick their brains.

Apart from the inimitable Mike Stimpson, I met Gareth Hardwick whom I had spoken with many times on the helpline of the Small Landlords

Association (SLA), now The National Landlords Association. It was Gareth who had encouraged me to start a landlords' association in the Midlands because, in those days, SLA hadn't the resources to deal with local issues. It was to Gareth that I turned when, running the AML helpline, I was asked questions that I could not answer. Gareth told me, "Don't worry, you will not be asked thousands of different questions, you will asked the same few questions thousands of times". This gave me the confidence to start the helpline for landlords in the Midlands that I operated for nine years and his words proved to be true – thank goodness. I quickly learned to go to the primary source for my information which was usually the original legislation. With no Google to help me in those days, I became very proficient at reading and absorbing information and disseminating the facts to other landlords.

There were so many characters around the NFRL table; I learned something from all of them, but there was one with whom I connected from day one, Ron Powell. He was the Vice Chair of NFRL and representative of Darlington Landlords' Association. I spent hours talking to Ron on the phone, and on our journeys to and from NFRL meetings. We argued like an old married couple, about many aspects of the business, but at the end of the day we shared a respect and fondness for each other, which lasted until the day that he died in 2004. I felt the loss dreadfully, my sparring partner, my mentor, my dear friend and the man that told me, "Inside every strong woman there is a little girl who just wants someone to put his arms around her and say, 'leave it to me'". I shall always miss Ron.

During my time on the Executive of NFRL the rumblings of new legislation began. I had never seen a piece of legislation develop from conception to birth, and I feel very privileged to have followed the Housing Act 2004 through this journey. I feel even more privileged to have been able to influence the content of the Act and, in particular, to have been chosen to represent NFRL in discussions about tenants' deposit protection (TDP). TDP was always going to be a bumpy ride for landlords because the law makers had once been students, and had remembered the landlords who had withheld their deposits 'without justification'.

Malcolm Turton, who later became the first CEO of NFRL, had accomplished considerable ground work on TDP. He had even tried to persuade associations, that were members of NFRL, to trial a voluntary scheme in order to avoid legislation but, when landlords failed to support the scheme, legislation was inevitable.

In 1998 Citizens Advice published *Unsafe Deposit*, a report describing how tens of thousands of private tenants were being cheated out of millions of pounds by unscrupulous landlords. The report called then for a statutory

Tenancy Deposit scheme to be set up, modelled on a successful scheme already running in Australia.

Citizens Advice successfully campaigned with housing charity Shelter, to get an amendment included in the Housing Bill to introduce such a scheme.

I remember listening to the parliamentary debate on the proposed TDP legislation at that time and thinking, "Oh my God! We are in big trouble!"

There was no time to lose; we had a battle on our hands. We spoke to landlords' representatives in New South Wales, home of the 'model' TDP scheme. Under their legislation, ALL tenants' deposits must be paid into a national holding account; the cost of the scheme was met by the interest made on the monies held. They warned us that landlords were waiting years for deposits to be returned to them, this was because tenants would not pay the last months' rent, then did not bother to sign out the deposit so that the landlord could recover his losses. As an aside the DPS (custodial scheme for England and Wales) quoted on the web site in Dec 2010:

"Despite an impressive £3m being returned, there remains £2m that is yet to be claimed and The DPS is appealing to tenants to step forward and re-claim these

deposits. "There is still a significant amount of unclaimed monies and tenants are missing out on money which is rightfully theirs. We are committed to repaying deposits as quickly as possible – and text message notification has helped enormously with this challenge but unfortunately some tenants are still not keeping their contact details up to date, putting their deposit in limbo," explained Mr Firth." [1]

Why do I find it so hard to believe that these deposits are all money that should go back to tenants? Maybe because I have heard so many stories from landlords and agents who cannot get the money back, despite having evidence that it is theirs by right.

Here is a story that was posted on one of the discussion forums that I take part in, *www.Propertytribes.com*, in September last year.

"Back in June one of my tenants passed away - I notified DPS and asked their advice re the deposit - I was told they would suspend this until the next of kin could be contacted. DPS told me I would need to get signed authorisation that the N.O.K was happy for the LL to have to deposit to cover cleaning and rent etc... I wrote this letter to the N.O.K with a section for her to sign.

The next of kin went back to her native country abroad and has been uncontactable since. DPS told me I would need to start a single claim process... I have done this, just as I was about to post this off to DPS the N.O.K. returns my signed letter of agreement, yay I call DPS and explain I now have their letter and what is my next step.

"Here is where my patience runs very thin..... The DPS now tell me that because the N.O.K. have been in touch they cannot now accept my single claim, the letter which THEY asked me to get is not valid and they do not know why I have it. The N.O.K would need to contact DPS direct to have the Deposit changed into her name.... why I ask as she did not rent the property? DPS have no answer.

"I ask.. "what if N.O.K wont contact you, what then?" oh you'll have to go to court and get a court order telling us to release the money! I asked the so called supervisor what the DPS policy was if there was no N.O.K what would happen? Surprisingly he had no answer." [sic]

We needed to devise an alternative that would enable landlords to satisfy the demands to protect tenants' deposits, while at the same time, enabling us to remain in control of the deposit and to recover justifiable losses quickly. I revisited the scheme that Malcolm Turton had tried to persuade us to use. With a little tweaking this was the scheme that I presented to John Daniels, then Senior Civil Servant, Department of the Environment, Transport and the Regions (DETR) now called Department for Communities and Local Government (DCLG). I had learned that one did not approach a Minister to bring about important changes, the correct route was via a Senior Civil Servant who would examine the proposals and advice the Minister. John Daniels was a really approachable man. On one occasion, at the Department for Communities and Local Government in Eland House, Westminster, while my heart was thumping in my chest, he made it very comfortable for me to explain the proposals to add another option to the TDP section of the Housing Bill.

I had explained to him what is now known as the *Insurance Scheme* in Section 212 of the Housing Act 2004. This gave landlords the choice of either putting their tenants' deposits into the custodial scheme, at no cost, or holding their tenants deposits. Having paid an Insurance Premium, it offered the tenant protection in the event that we could not agree on liabilities at the end of the tenancy. It would seem that the Scottish Parliament were not convinced that this was a good option because it does not appear in their DTP legislation covered by The Tenancy Deposit Schemes (Scotland) Regulations 2011. The regulations require that the deposit must be paid to an approved scheme administrator and that the deposit is held in an approved scheme for the duration of the tenancy; the same scheme that is used in New South Wales!

I continue to follow the journey of deposit protection legislation, which in my opinion, has lost its way and is now more about taking legal action against landlords who make administrative errors, than about protection the tenants' rights. I will always be proud of the fact that I was able to influence the drafting of legislation, and to soften the edges, by giving landlords a choice.

I now have only two remaining colleagues from my early days with NRFL, John Socha, who transformed the SLA into the NLA and still represents them in Northampton, and Patrick Jacobs, Financial Director of NLA. These two men were determined to have just one major organisation to represent the PRS in the UK. We enjoyed many a heated discussion around the table because we all held strong opinions, and cared very much about the future of the private rented sector. We no longer partake in debates of this nature because we are on the same team now. In 2007 I realised that the time for local landlords associations had passed; it was time for us all to become part of one central organisation, with branches throughout the UK. John and Patrick had been right; AML became part of NLA, and I became the NLA Regional Representative for the West Midlands.

I worked in the 'real world' until December 1980, holding a Sales Management post within the newspaper industry. The then family owned company had a strong belief that you could only expect employees to do a good job if you offered them the knowledge and training to do so. The job I had enjoyed most on my way up the ladder was *Training Officer*. The company invested heavily in my personal training and development for the post; I really loved taking a person who had never done the job before, and helping them become the best that they could be. The joy of sharing in the success of my 'trainees' gave me a satisfaction that had been hard to find in anything I did later. When the thirty-three London boroughs realised that they needed private landlords to help to prevent the increase of homelessness, they knew that they would need a way of ensuring that those landlords knew their job. *London Landlords Accreditation Scheme* (LLAS), now *UK Landlord Accreditation Partnership* (UKLAP), was born. The local authorities, working with the NLA, devised a one day programme. It had all the information that landlords would need to enable them to deal with legislation, regulation, communication and documentation. I was delighted when my application, to deliver that information to landlords, was accepted. I was also very proud to be the first person to deliver an LLAS seminar. I began to see the difference between the landlords at the end of the seminar, and those who had walked into the room at the start of the day. Many of these landlords had been in business for several years and had a good working knowledge. Others were fairly new to the business, but at the end of the seminar they all shared one thing; they were confident that if they came into contact with an *Environmental Health Officer* (EHO), Fire Officer, or indeed anyone with the power to take action against them, should they be failing to meet current regulations and legislation, they were on a level playing field. Knowledge really is power.

I am a founder member of *Homestamp*; the only consortium of its kind in the UK, where local authorities, fire, police, landlords, landlords' organisations, universities, students' unions and other partners, work together to find solutions to problems in the PRS in the West Midlands. I decided that I would introduce the concept of LLAS to my colleagues. Some of them were sceptical at first, one EHO said, "Landlords will not pay and spend a day learning". After a very stressful day, where I demonstrated the content of the seminar to them, they were prepared to give it a try. I am very proud of my landlord and letting agent colleagues because since we began in 2007, more that 2,000 of them have attended those seminars, and have subsequently become accredited by *Midlands Landlord Accreditation Scheme* (MLAS). As more landlords and agents fill the seminars every month, that number grows significantly. I have delivered a seminar, with similar content, over two hundred times now. Each time it is made different by the questions and discussions that take place, among the landlords and letting agents, in the room. I have also delivered more *Continual Professional Development* (CPD) seminars than I care to count; the satisfaction I get from this work makes me 'buzz' for hours. I am currently the Vice Chair of *Homestamp* and I am very proud of the work my colleagues and I have done, and continue to do, to ensure the PRS is, and remains, a happy place for both tenants to live, and good landlords to thrive. Equipping landlords to do an effective and responsible job, in my opinion, is the best thing that we have ever done.

I have travelled a long way since I first became a green landlord in 1972. I never stop learning and I have never stopped loving the job that I do. I have fallen down many of the potholes in the road, but each of my, often expensive, mistakes have made me a better landlord and helped me to protect my investments. One day I may stand back and let others manage my properties, but until that day, I am content being a very hands on landlord and property investor.

I want to end with a great quote from a landlord for whom I have the utmost respect. Thank you, Jonathan Clark, for putting into words my own philosophy.

"My tenants are paying for my financial freedom and I do everything in my power to give them the freedom to enjoy the homes that I provide"

INTRODUCTION

"I will tell you how to become rich. Close the doors. Be fearful when others are greedy. Be greedy when others are fearful." - Warren Buffet

Anything that happens to one tenant group will have a knock-on effect with all other tenant groups. Landlords cannot afford to be myopic, "I don't take tenants who..." In my experience the tenant who moves in is often very different to the tenant who moves out, and bad tenants are not easily avoided. Our financial freedom is in the hands of our tenants and those who have the power' to have an impact on our business investments.

They say that money changes people, but the lack of money changes people far more. Landlords are seen as the idle rich and we may suffer from this misnomer in the next couple of years. We are already seeing a huge increase in rent arrears from tenants who think that we can afford it 'better than they can'. Local authorities 'fund raising' with the introduction of *Selective Licensing*, and crazy increases in HMO licence and renewal fees. Shelter is fighting to reduce fees for tenants and increase their security of tenure. Banks no longer feel that property is 'as safe as houses' and are increasing the cost of borrowing, and tightening their criteria; one bank is even increasing rates on existing loans. Government is reducing the amount a tenant can claim in housing benefits. HMRC are not going to be left out of the party and plan to introduce what is known as the *General Anti-Abuse Rule* (GAAR)..............

I don't want to be the prophet of doom; I am generally a very positive person, but I feel more vulnerable now than I have since I started letting property in 1972. I have worked very hard for my financial security and, like many other landlords, have taken risks and invested time and money in a bid to ensure that I am safe in my final years. I now see the vultures circling overhead and my present 'building project' is a Nissen hut. Once I have finished the construction, I will share my 'building plans' with other landlords – apart from the many who are so happy looking back at the property market, that they fail to see what is ahead. It is not my intention to 'put down' or 'put off' those who are investing in property, I just want to present what I see so that we are all able to prepare contingency plans. I have seen too many people investing in property who have no idea what it is to be a landlord – many of them do not think of themselves as 'landlords' and will instead refer to themselves as a "property investor". We are all property investors, but if we are receiving rent from those investments then we are, in law, landlords, and we need to be aware of the pit falls in our road to financial security.

"In a time of drastic change it is the learners who inherit the future. The learned usually find themselves equipped to live in a world that no longer exists". - *Eric Hoffer*

MARY LATHAM

1.

THE DANGER OF BUYING A PROPERTY FOR CONVERSION TO A HOUSE IN MULTIPLE OCCUPATION (HMO)

"Romney shot himself in the foot this week, then re-loaded, and shot the other foot" – *Affan Chowdhry*

Most universities were built before most of us were born, and just like Airports, it is fairly safe to assume that if you buy your home close to one of them, there is the potential for it to be very noisy at times. I would not live close to a university - while I appreciate my student tenants, I certainly would not want to be woken at 3am, as they walk home from the student union bars. I cannot understand why a person would choose to live in an area where there is a particularly strong potential for issues of this nature to arise. Unless the issues do not concern them?

Article 4 Direction was the Government's way of appeasing voters who do not want to live close to students. The vernacular *'studentification'* has crept into use in recent years. It is a colloquialism used to describe areas where former family homes have been converted into student accommodation or *Homes/Houses in Multi Occupation* (HMO's). As the student community grew, owner occupiers began to resent what they deemed an intrusion of students into their communities; they responded by putting pressure on local authorities to control/curb the increase in properties that were being converted into HMO's.

Planning Use Classes:

- Use Class C3 (Dwelling Houses) – These generally include self contained houses or flats occupied by a single person, a couple or a family.
- Use Class C4 (Small HMOs) – These include self contained houses and flats shared by between 3 and 6 unrelated people.

Bedsits, larger shared houses, and flats, those occupied by more than six unrelated people, do not fall within a *Planning Use Class*. Planning permission is required for changes to these uses.

As the last Government were on their way out, on April 6th 2010, they put in place a change to planning regulations, it stipulated that any property with established use as a Class C3, where the owner wanted to use it as a Class C4, planning consent would have to be requested. The new Government quickly modified this, enabling local authorities to enforce the regulation, but only if they believed it was particularly necessary, and only after they had consulted the other property owners in the specific area. Finally, the *Article 4 Direction* must be publicised for consultation, and one year's notice will be required before it is brought into effect.

Although the split of residential property into two separate classes remained. From 1 October 2010, a change of use from a Class C3 to Class C4, and vice versa, was once again possible, and planning permission was no longer required - unless the local authority had put an *Article 4 Direction* in place in that area. They did this by allowing authorities to withdraw the 'permitted development' rights, which would otherwise apply by virtue of the Town and Country Planning (General Permitted Development) Order 1995 as amended (the 'GDPO'). An *Article 4 Direction* does not prevent the development to which it applies, but instead specifies that planning permission must first be obtained from the local planning authority for that development. In the case of conservation areas, this process allows for the consideration of the impact, of the proposed development, on the character and appearance of the conservation area.

The definition of different planning use classes are set out in the Town and Country Planning (Use Classes) Order 1987 (as amended).

Many landlords confuse 'change of use' with physical changes to the building. Where an *Article 4 Direction* is in place, one does not need to make any physical changes to the building, this is simply about how the building is occupied. If the property is occupied by three to six unrelated people, who are sharing facilities, it is a Class C4. Larger HMO's (Six tenants and more) must always have planning consent.

Some cautions:

1. Some local authorities are asking for proof of up to 10 years of established use as an HMO, in order to avoid an *Article 4 Direction* and the need for a planning application, while others accept a Tenancy Agreement that was in place prior to the Direction coming into force, as proof of established use. This could

mean that an established HMO is refused permission when the landlord cannot prove established use for the required time.

2. If a property, that has established use as a HMO, changes use to a family home, this will break the established use, and will need planning consent to be used as a HMO again in future.

3. If you are considering buying a property for conversion, in an established student area, check the local authority web site to see if there are any plans to put an *Article 4 Direction* in the area.

4. If lenders become aware that there is an *Article 4 Direction* in place, in an area where you are planning to buy a property for conversion to an HMO, they may refuse your loan.

In my opinion, many disgruntled residents who have pressurised their local authorities into introducing *Article 4 Direction's* in their areas, have not taken into consideration the adverse affect it is likely to have on the value of their homes. In an area where there is already a high proportion of student HMO's, the houses are desired by landlords with the intention of converting them into more student HMO's. Landlords have driven up the cost of properties in these areas despite the downturn in property prices generally. The rental income from a HMO in the right area makes this type of property very attractive to investors. If landlords are not certain that they will be able to use a property as a HMO, they will not buy the property. If families don't want to live there, and landlords won't take the risk, who will buy these properties when they come onto the market? This is bound to have a negative impact on the value of the property. The horse has already bolted in most student areas and control of the spread of HMOs is about 10 years too late. In my opinion *Article 4 Direction's* will have a very short shelf life, and in the meantime, those of us who own established HMO's, will see an increase in their value because investors will know that they have established use and are therefore a safe investment.

Changes to Housing Benefits rules reduced the amount paid to a single person, under the age of thirty-five years, to the rate for a room in a shared house, where previously, if they were over twenty-five years, they would have been entitled to claim the self contained home rate. This change has had a major impact on many landlords, who were forced to take a reduction of up to 50% in their rent, or evict the tenant because of his inability to pay the full amount. The benefit for landlords who let HMO's was that there was an increase in the number of people who wanted to rent a room in the property. This meant many landlords invested in HMO's in order to meet the increased demand. An *Article 4 Direction* is not specifically about student

HMO's. Where there is a *'Direction* in place, landlords will not buy properties to convert into HMO's for any tenant group, because they cannot afford to risk being refused planning consent; this has already had a negative impact on the supply of affordable homes. All local authorities are struggling to house the homeless, and single people under the age of 35 years are a particularly difficult group for them to house because they simply haven't enough stock of small homes. People on modest incomes are also attracted to HMO's, and if they cannot find an affordable home, they often cannot take up employment in an area. This in turn will have an impact on businesses and services that depend on staff who are paid a modest wage. Without investment from private landlords, the quantity of affordable home that are needed, cannot be met. Landlords are already reducing the amount of homes they make available to people on benefits because of concerns relating to the *Welfare Reform* and *Universal Credit.* Any local authority that compounds the problem with the use of an *Article 4 Direction,* is indeed 're-aiming the gun at the other foot'. Just how long it will take for 'the penny to drop' remains to be seen.

MARY LATHAM

2.

CAN GOVERNMENT REALLY AFFORD TO ALLOW THE BUY-TO-LET MARKET COLLAPSE BECAUSE THE LENDERS HAVE LOST THEIR NERVE?

"The human species, according to the best theory I can form of it, is composed of two distinct races, the men who borrow and the men who lend." - Charles Lamb

Finance is not my 'strong suit', and I am at the stage in my landlord journey where I am no longer buying, but since the supply of money has a direct effect on property values, I take a keen interest in anything that may have an impact on a person's ability to raise finance for the purpose of purchasing property. I will not even attempt to draw conclusions from that which I have observed. However, I do wish to make you aware of what it is that I have seen, with the intention of enabling you to draw your own conclusions, and to plan accordingly.

"Britain is issuing the largest number of 'landlord loans' since records began, official figures have revealed.

"One in eight mortgages is now a buy-to-let loan deal - an all-time high.

"Of the 11.3million mortgages in this country, 1.44million are buy-to-let loans, rather than standard residential mortgages.

"A decade ago, there were only 275,500 buy-to-let loans, equal to just 2.4 per cent of the entire market.

"Today the number of buy-to-let loans is equal to 12.7 per cent [of the entire market], according to the figures from the Council of Mortgage Lenders." [2]

Lenders appear to misunderstand HMO Licensing and landlords, who hold an HMO Licence, are finding it difficult to re-finance the building, or indeed to raise funds to buy a licenced HMO. Speaking to landlords recently it seems that even those who have un-licensable HMO's are being offered lower loan to value lending; 70% appears to be the norm.

A spokesman for RBS subsidiary NatWest Intermediary Solutions stated:

"I can confirm that it is our current policy, and has been for some time, to not accept applications for buy-to-let mortgages where the landlord requires a selective licence"

My investigations into why Banks should suddenly be averse to HMO's, led me to this.

"In what may be described as an attempt to prevent careless property–backed lending, the Financial Services Authority (FSA) has threatened to impose 'slotting' rules on banks in the UK, to instruct them as to how they should assess the risk of their portfolios of property–backed loans. Penningtons banking and finance partner Malcolm Pearson examines these proposals in Estates Gazette:

"In 2007, the FSA outlined five criteria of slotting, under the Basel II banking regime, and attached various risk weightings to each. Stemming from the remains of the UK's economy post credit crunch, the plans to introduce the slotting rules form part of a global effort to prevent banks from understating the risks involved in lending.

"In essence, the FSA's basic reasoning seems morally sound. Nevertheless, imposing such an

unsophisticated strategy on the complex, multifaceted banking system, and expecting it to succeed having only just risen from the ashes of the financial crisis, seems recklessly optimistic.

"Crude and prescriptive

"Slotting involves assigning new and existing loans to proposed categories; consisting of just five slots under the FSA criteria, the risk weighting is as set out in the table below:

Less than 2.5 years	50%	70%	115%	250%	0%
2.5 years or more	70%	90%	115%	250%	0%

"Owing to the 9% equity ratio arising from the Basel III global banking code, a bank that lends £100bn is required to have at least £9bn of its own. The remaining £91bn belongs to depositors at the bank, including private customers, pension funds and corporate treasurers. These figures dictate the percentages for the FSA's suggested slots in the table, meaning even the best-performing loan of less than 2.5 years would require the bank to allocate £4.50 for every £100 of loan (9% x 50%) and £6.30 (9% x 70%) for a loan of 2.5 years or more.

"Not all banks are reckless and not all investors are high-risk, despite the impending possibility of having a property classified as such." *[3]*

This is what is said in the Document *"Slotting Criteria for Specialised Lending"* Produced by Financial Services Authority:

*"'Income-producing real estate 226'. Income-producing real estate (IPRE) refers to a method of providing funding to real estate (such as, office buildings to let, retail space, **multifamily residential buildings**, industrial or warehouse space, and hotels) where the prospects for repayment and recovery on the exposure depend primarily on the cash flows generated by the asset. The primary source of these cash flows would generally be lease or rental payments or the sale of the asset. The borrower may be, but is not required to be, an SPE, an operating company focused on real estate construction or holdings, or an operating company with sources of revenue other than real estate. The distinguishing characteristic of IPRE versus other corporate exposures that are collateralised by real estate is the strong positive correlation between the prospects for repayment of the exposure and the prospects for recovery in the event of default, with both depending primarily on the cash flows generated by a property."* [4]

Written in December 2011, this explains what the Slotting Criteria is all about:

"The Financial Services Authority is forcing UK banks to reassess the riskiness of their commercial

real estate loan books or use its 'slotting' rules.
The Bank of England and the FSA are uneasy about banks' internal models for calculating the credit risks of commercial property loans and believe they are not setting aside enough regulatory capital to cover the risks. "The FSA feel people are applying the regime relatively aggressively and getting capital weightings lower than they should be," said one banker. "All banks are being told their internal models are inadequate and the only alternative is slotting." Industry insiders say the move to make all banks slot their loans according to the FSA's criteria mean risk weighting will inevitably be more conservative and require them to put more capital aside. This could reduce the amount and raise the price of lending to commercial real estate, they say. But the FSA has backed off introducing new, more prescriptive guidance that could have forced banks to reclassify a huge swathe of loans as 'weak' and assign a penal 250% risk weighting to them. This could have dramatically increased the amount of capital banks had to hold against their portfolios, weakening their balance sheets, restricting new lending and increasing margins."

The article concludes with:

"Regulators are keeping a close eye on the industry's risk weightings and real estate loan provisioning. The FSA recently reported to the Bank of England on UK banks' 'extend and

pretend' strategy on non-market terms; a June survey it carried out found the UK's six major banks were applying this to almost £50bn of loans. UK banks' corporate loan books are heavily focused on real estate lending and "deleveraging has progressed more slowly than elsewhere, partly reflecting the large-scale forbearance on corporate real estate loans." [5]

I am wondering if the term "**multifamily residential buildings**" has caused the banks to 'back off' licenced HMO's, and that it is this, not the fact that they are licenced, per se? Could this also lead to problems of financing non-licensable HMO's in future or in fact buildings which have been converted into self contained flats?

While fully acknowledging that I am not a financial specialist, I am a specialist in the residential property market, and venture to share my opinion, regarding the criteria that I would apply, should I be considering loaning funds to an individual whose desire was to buy property for the purpose of letting.

- Does this person know the law and regulation related to the business? Have they invested their time and money to achieve an accreditation through an education based scheme?
- Has this person got sufficient funds, borrowed or otherwise, to bring the property up to the *Decent Homes*

Standard, or higher, should the market demand? Can they meet all the legal requirements before the property is let?

- Have they done the necessary homework; is there a market for the property they propose to let, in the area where they plan to buy?
- Is there any regulation in place that the landlord is not aware of, *Article 4 Direction's*, *Selective Licensing*, *planning controls*, or *lease restrictions*, etc?
- Will the property return a positive cash flow, one that will cover the loan, keep the property up to standard, pay Agency fees (if the property is going to be managed by an Agent), pay on-going letting fees/marketing costs, and also leave a margin for rent arrears and the cost of removing a tenant if necessary?
- Does this person understand how to legally remove an undesirable tenant, and do they realise length of time this might take? Do they possess a 'financial safety net' which will cover the loss of income during this period?
- Is he/she a member of an organisation that can supply the correct documents and support, to sustain the tenancy?
- Has this person got a system in place to ensure that he/she remains legally compliant at all times, thus avoiding expensive litigation, which may result in

large fines and rent repayment orders for up to one year's rent or up to four times the tenant's deposit, etc?

- Do they have *Rent Guarantee Insurance, Public Liability Insurance, Landlord Property Insurance,* and (provided the property is furnished) *Contents Insurance?*
- Does this person wish to manage their own property, or will they employ a Letting Agent? If the intention is to employ a Letting Agent, how will a reputable one, particularly one with *Client Money Protection,* be decided upon? Is he/she aware that they cannot devolve their legal responsibilities to that Agent?
- Have provisions been made to re-pay an interest only loan, should the property value decrease?

Are Banks aware of these important issues, or are they making a risk assessments based purely on FSA criteria, without taking into consideration the 'real' risks of investing in property to let? Letting property is not a passive investment; traditional investment criteria are only part of the picture.

There has been some controversy about lending to the landlords who are willing to let to tenants on benefits, or those accepting tenants from local authorities. In December 2012, one lender, the

largest lender catering for landlords who
provide housing to those in receipt of housing
benefit, had changed its terms and conditions;
they had excluded landlords who wanted to offer
properties to these tenants. It did not last for
long; in March 2013 their Mortgage Director
announced:

*"The clarification of the terms and conditions,
which took place last December, brought us into
line with several other Buy-to-Let lenders," he
said. "This will now be removed."*

*""The Buy-to-Let sector is very important to us,"
he went on. "We have listened to concerns that
have been expressed by some of our customers,
over the last few days, and believe this is the right
way forward for us, for landlords and for their
tenants."*

It is, however, clear that lenders are concerned
about the forth coming changes in *Welfare
Reform,* and in particular, the fact that *Universal
Credit* will prevent most landlords from being
paid, without having to rely on the tenant to pass
the benefits on.

If landlords cannot get funding to provide
affordable homes, the supply will be reduced at a
time when they were never more needed. *Article
4 Directions* and *Selective Licensing* are already
having an adverse affect on the supply; I have
covered these separately.

From 1st May 2013 The Bank of Ireland 'moved the goal posts' for existing borrowers, announcing that their new differential rate on tracker mortgages will be increased from 1.75% to 4.49%, plus bank base of 0.5%, a new rate of 4.99%. The bank informed 13,500 lenders that they would expected to pay the increase, those lenders have confirmed that over half of the customers affected are on buy-to-let mortgages. Of the total number of customers affected, around 80% have an LTV of 60% or less. The FSA decided that there was no case to answer and this did not please the Treasury. I imagine their main concern is that other banks may follow suit.

On 28 Mar 2013 the Telegraph reported:

"Martin Wheatley, soon to take up his position as Chief Executive of the Financial Conduct Authority (FCA), has been ordered by the Treasury Select Committee (TSC)to give more information on Bank of Ireland's decision.

"The TSC said a letter from Mr Wheatley explaining the current regulator's actions did not "address the main issues".

"Your response does not tell the Committee whether you were concerned at the action of the Bank of Ireland, what assessment you have made of the impact its decision might be on the rest of the industry, nor how the FCA would act in the event of lenders taking this sort of action in the

future," wrote Andrew Tyrie MP, Chairman of the Committee, in a letter to Mr Wheatley"

Mark Alexander, a Landlord since 1989 and founder of *Property118.com* and *Money Center*, had this to say:

"Property118 will be taking legal advice from Justin Selig of The Law Department on Tuesday next on whether we should instruct barristers to proceed now with a class action, or await the second response from the FSA to the Treasury Select Committee letter from Andrew Tyrie. Justin Selig has kindly sent me copies of the FSA response and the subsequent letter to the FSA from Martin Wheatley MP. I have to say, the questions in the second letter are far stronger and more direct than the first. It seems quite clear to me that Mr. Tyrie believes the BoI contract terms to be unfair and he's looking for the FSA to agree the same. The FSA response will be very interesting indeed."

Mortgage Express, now part of *UK Asset Resolution Limited* (UKAR), which are now owned by Government are actively reducing their lending; one of the ways that they are accomplishing this is by using their *Right to Consolidate*. This means that if a borrower wants to repay one of his mortgages, they can force him to repay all of his mortgages with them. There has always been a clause in their terms, which gives them the right to do this, but, until 2011, they did not invoke this condition. Now they state that any surplus, gathered from the proceeds of a sale after repayment of the mortgage, is to be paid towards other mortgages, otherwise they will force the repayment of all of them.

In 2011 they were offering landlords, who are existing borrowers, the opportunity to switch to new terms with a 3.99% fixed rate for 7 years, but at the end of the term the loan must be repaid.

In the half year accounts to July 2012 they repaid £700m in Government loans from the *Mortgage Express* (Bradford & Bingley) income.

Yet another issue is that of the many landlords who have interest-only loans - these were commonly available until early in 2012. The *Council of Mortgage Lenders* figures show that interest-only mortgages accounted for 33% of all mortgages taken out in 2007. The FSA says:

"80% of these have no repayment strategy in place, and with lenders clamping down, many of these borrowers, now approaching retirement, could be forced to sell their homes."

Most landlords depend on an increase in the value of a property, and few intend to pay their loans before eventually selling up. It is common practice for landlords to keep their portfolio highly geared, re-mortgaging regularly to pull out the cash for the next deposit. This strategy is highly effective provided interest rates are low, rents are high and interest-only loans are available. I have talked about the future of rents elsewhere.

On the subject of rents:

"Buy-to-let mortgage applications are failing because surveyors are 'down valuing' the rental income and advising lenders accordingly.

"In some cases, they are even down valuing the rent already being received.

"The claims come in a article in The Sunday Times, which reports that some lenders are rejecting landlords' rental estimates.

"Most lenders want to see monthly mortgage repayments covered by rent with a 25% excess, to cover expenditure and void periods. Some lenders want to see 130% of rental cover, while others are happy with 100%.

"Down valuing the rent could mean either outright rejection of the application, or that a lender will cap the amount they will lend to well under the borrower's expectations."

And as if there was not enough to concern us, another monster has reared its head.

According to new research, up to 1.43 million

homes in England and Wales are at risk from shortening leasehold terms, leaving borrowers and lenders with the prospect of negative equity.

The report from *e.surv*, the largest chartered surveyor in the UK, points out that the value of a home begins to drop dramatically, once a lease term reaches eighty years, and many lenders are unwilling to approve a mortgage on such properties. Once the lease reaches sixty years the value can plummet even further.

The research estimates that this situation could affect 10.1% of residential housing stock, this amounts to around 1.43 million homes worth £2.2 billion.

Of particular concern are leasehold flats, which account for 817,000 of the 1.43 million leasehold properties in the UK. When there is only eighty years left on the lease, the value of the property begins to fall. Once the lease is down to sixty-five years, most lenders will refuse to offer a mortgage on the property, meaning only a cash buyer would have the means to purchase it, and he/she would most likely expect a generous discount in order to do so. If we combine this with the number of interest only mortgages, which are held on 14% of all properties purchased in the last decade, this means that regardless of what happens to property values, generally the erosion of value caused by a shortening lease will mean that the property may be worth less than the outstanding loan. This could take us back to the days before the *Leasehold Reform Act 1967*, when many people lost their homes after the lease came to an end, and they had no legal right to extend the lease or purchase the freehold. In fact, even after the Act, many people with high value properties lost them because they were outside of the scope of the Act.

How long will it be before the lenders see this as a new way to reduce their mortgage books or the term of the loan on a leasehold property?

There are some questions we need to consider.

- Will the interest rates continue to remain low? If so, will landlords be able to continue to access cheap lending at a decent loan to value for all types of properties with all client groups?
- Will more lenders increase the differential between the base rate and the rate charged on tracker mortgages?
- Will the lenders offer an affordable replacement when our current interest-only deals run out?
- Will more lenders decrease their exposure by calling in loans using the "small print'?

- Will the new FCA take action against lenders who have 'unfair terms' in their loan agreements?
- Can Government really afford to allow the buy-to-let and indeed the whole UK property market collapse because the lenders have lost their nerve?

I will leave the last word to Martin Wheatley, a director of the *Financial Services Authority* (FSA), and the Chief Executive designate of the new *Financial Conduct Authority* (FCA), who spoke of his *"concern over the 'ticking time-bomb' of 1.5 million mortgages, worth a colossal £120bn, which will come to an end over the next 10 years".*

MARY LATHAM

3.

A RISK TO CONSIDER WHEN BUYING BELOW MARKET VALUE (BMV)

"All that glisters is not gold; Often have you heard that told: Many a man his life hath sold" – *William Shakespeare.*

Many investors have made money, at least on paper, by buying property at below market value (BMV). This works regardless of the property market, and many investors rely on the built in equity of these properties to finance their next purchase, by refinancing them and pulling out the equity. Some investors 'flip' the property, which means that they buy at a low price, then resell in a short space of time, either having carried out a 'prima facie' refurbishment, or often without doing anything at all.

There are pitfalls to this strategy if landlords are actively targeting 'distressed' sellers through advertising, mail shots, and bill boards. If the seller becomes bankrupt within five years of the sale, the sale can be reversed. If the property was subsequently sold for a higher price, within a short space of time, this is likely to be taken as evidence that the original purchase price was too low.

The same is true of *Exchange with Delayed Completion* or *Lease Option* contracts. Sale and rent back agreements are now regulated by the *Financial Services Authority* (FSA), and if the person remains in the property before the option is completed, *Lease Option* sales are also regulated by the FSA. [6]

This is not something new, but what is new is the increase in the number of private individuals who are declaring themselves bankrupt. This is how it works:

"Fast-track Voluntary Arrangements

"Fast-track Voluntary Arrangements (FTVAs) are a way to deal with your debts if you've already been made bankrupt. They're an agreement where your assets are sold to pay your debts and your bankruptcy is annulled (cancelled).

"Get an FTVA

"You can only get an FTVA if you've already been made bankrupt by the court.

1. *Contact the Official Receiver (an officer of the bankruptcy court).*
2. *They'll send you an FTVA application form and tell you what you need to do – for example, provide details of your assets.*
3. *Send your FTVA application to the Official Receiver.*
4. *If the Official Receiver accepts your FTVA application they'll ask your creditors to accept it.*
5. *The FTVA starts if 75% of the creditors who respond accept it. It will apply to all your creditors, including any who disagreed to it.*

"What happens next?

"When you get the FTVA:

- *the court order making you bankrupt is annulled (cancelled)*
- *any assets not already sold or needed to pay your debts are returned to you*
- *your FTVA is added to the Individual Insolvency Register - it's removed 3 months after the FTVA ends"* [7]

"Entering into a transaction at an under value" means 'giving items away', or 'selling them' at less than their true value. It is a myth that you can give away your possessions just before bankruptcy in an attempt to exclude them. Any transaction can be reversed with a Court Order.

If, before bankruptcy, a person sells their interest in any asset to anyone for less than its true worth, the Trustee may apply to the court for an order to reverse the sale. The Trustee can apply to the court and have the transaction reversed if either of the following is true.

- The transaction was performed up to five years before the bankruptcy, and you were insolvent at the time.
- The transaction was performed up to two years before bankruptcy.

The *Official Receiver* can look at sales of assets going back five years. They check to see if sales were made for less than the true value of the asset, this is based on the assumption that unscrupulous people offload their valuables, declare themselves bankrupt, and then buy them back at a cost that is below the true value.

Buying at auction is probably the safest option, but many buyers advertise/leaflet offering a quick sale to a *distressed seller,* and this could be dangerous.

Debt levels currently peak around the time that people turn 40, but the *Consumer Credit Counselling Service* says its research suggests consumers are building up large levels of debt at a much younger age.

"Almost three quarters of people aged 18 to 39 have unsecured debts, compared with around 60% of the 40-54 age group. We should therefore assume that a person can be declared bankrupt at any age, regardless of their situation.

"Mortgage lenders are becoming very wary of lending to buy property at below market value from "distressed sellers"

"To assess the risks of a further slump, we track two measures of valuation. The first is the price-to-income ratio, a gauge of affordability. The second is the price-to-rent ratio, which is a bit like the price-to-earnings ratio used to value companies."

There was a recent case where a Housing Association assisted a family who were in financial difficulties, they did this by buying their home and enabling them to continue to live there. Shortly after the sale the family went into voluntary bankruptcy. The *Official Receiver* overturned the sale because the property was sold below market value; the Housing Association, and their lender, lost the property.[8]

It was announced in April 2013 that *The Office of Fair Trading* (OFT) is investigating fears that people, desperate for money, are being preyed on by firms offering 'quick house sales'.

Fifty unidentified companies operating in the market, have been contacted by the watchdog for details on their business models, while consumers are being urged to contact the OFT with information on their experiences.

Firms in the sector offer to buy a house themselves, or find someone else to snap it up, often for less than the full market value of the property.

The OFT states that...

"...while such companies may offer a 'valuable service' for people who need fast access to cash, it is concerned that stressed and vulnerable home owners looking for a way out of financial difficulties could be misled into selling for far less than their home is worth."

There have been suggestions that some customers have been told at the final stage of the "quick sale" process that the price they were getting had been considerably reduced.

Other practices that the watchdog is looking out for include, firms hiding their fees behind initial valuations, which appear to offer a good price, and severe penalties for breach of contract.

More than 157,900 UK households had fallen behind on their mortgage payments by the end of 2012, and over 110,000 couples divorced in 2011 in England and Wales.

The OFT plans to publish a report on the quick house sale sector in July 2013.

Many lenders are now including questions about the financial status of the seller in their Mortgage Applications, and buyers would be well advised to look into this before they proceed with a purchase.

Buying from a 'motivated' seller differs greatly to buying from 'distressed' seller. People are often motivated to sell quickly at a low price because they need to change location, or because their domestic circumstance have changed. It is the seller who is facing repossession, or is in financial difficulties, that can cause concern. We all want to buy at the best possible price, but a 'bargain' is only a 'bargain' if it is a safe purchase.

4.

INSURANCE IS A GOOD INVESTMENT

"Misfortunes one can endure--they come from outside, they are accidents. But to suffer for one's own faults--ah!--there is the sting of life."
- Oscar Wilde

There are, of course, many types of Insurance that landlords can buy to protect themselves from unexpected events. Akin to most landlords, I hope to waste every penny spent on insurance, but I would not be without it, and I am always surprised when landlords tell me that they cannot afford to be fully insured.

Without venturing into the entire subject of insurance, I'd just like to highlight some of the issues that need to be considered.

We should all be covered for *Public Liability,* and if we have specific landlords insurance, this will be included. Those of us letting leasehold flats are paying our insurance for the building as part of our Service Charge, **Public Liability insurance is not usually included,** and we need to take out the extra cover. The cost of *Public Liability* insurance is very low, around £1 a week for a two bed roomed flat, and it is, of course, tax deductable.

It is essential for landlords to confirm with every contractor operating within a rented property, that they have suitable *Public Liability* cover. For instance, should they leave an item 'lying around', and a tenant or visitor is consequently harmed as a direct result, the claim should be made against their insurance, not ours! If they themselves are harmed, we want to avoid them claiming against us, unless it is our negligence that has caused the problem.

Some insurance policies exclude certain tenant groups, and some exclude tenants that have not been chosen by the landlord or a Letting Agent appointed by the landlord. Check your policy if you are considering signing a *Lease Agreement* with a local authority or other organisation. If they have nomination rights on the tenants who live in your properties, your insurance may not cover you.

There is a case currently moving through the courts, where a child was visiting a tenant, and was seriously injured on the stair case. Fortunately the landlord in this case was fully insured, but the insurance company has estimated that the legal costs alone will amount to more than £100,000, and the loss of earnings, and cost of care for the rest of the child's life, could amount to millions of pounds. Since most of us hold the ownership of our rented properties in our own name, rather than through a *Limited Liability Company*, we could lose everything we own in the event of a successful claim against us.

There are several things that we are obligated to do in order for our tenants to receive cover for their belongings. Some insurance companies insist that locks must be attached to each bedroom door in what is now an HMO, but was once a shared house (pre-Housing Act 2004). This is causing Council Tax issues in some areas. I have covered this separately. Some tenant groups find that the cost of insurance is very high and this is particularly true for students who are living in high density student areas, where burglaries take place more frequently. Often we can help them to reduce the cost by fitting alarms and exterior lighting.

It is important for landlords to have a clause in their Tenancy Agreements stipulating that a tenant must refrain from doing anything that could invalidate the insurance. A good example of this might be a policy that withdraws cover after a property has been empty for thirty days. It is important for tenants to keep us informed, should they plan to go away for longer than this period, in order for us to make the relevant enquires, with the insurance company, and find out what is required of us to ensure that we remain covered. The use of certain types of heater may be another example and, in particular, the use of portable heaters with 'gas' bottles.

Rent Guarantee Insurance (RGI) is now more affordable, and probably more necessary, than ever. Rent arrears have increased enormously in recent years, and the introduction of *Universal Credit*, for those tenants who need benefits to pay all or part of their rent, relationship breakdowns, and ill health, are likely to increase the risk of further rent arrears. RGI can only be bought when a full Credit Reference has been carried out and there are some tenants who will not pass this reference. There are some client groups, particularly those who rely on benefits to pay their rent, who do not qualify for RGI cover.

RGI not only provides cover when tenants fail to pay their rent, but the RGI company will take the necessary action to assist in the recovery of their losses, and where necessary, can have the tenant removed from the property. This not only eradicates the risk of losing income, but prevents landlords having to go through the long, and very often stressful, legal Possession Proceedings.

Some of the most positive news I have ascertained this year came from *LandlordReferencing.co.uk.* In partnership with *Experian*, they now offer a full credit reference, not to mention, a lifestyle reference, at a cost of only £4.99. Lifestyle referencing is becoming increasingly more important because it is not always those who cannot afford to, who do not pay their rent, but some tenants simply do not priorities rent and consequently choose to spend their money on other things. A lifestyle reference will distinguish these tenants when a conventional credit reference may not.

We should not choose to reduce our overheads by not covering accidental damage caused by tenants. In the event of a deposit dispute, it may be argued that the damage was accidental and could have been covered by insurance. If the landlord has chosen not to take the insurance cover, he may be said to have underwritten the damage himself. Beware of taking a high excess. In my experience most accidental damage amounts to less than £300, having a high excess means that many landlords find themselves paying for much of the damage themselves.

Arguably insurance can be considered the most necessary overhead – to risk not being fully insured is tantamount to leaping from a plane without a parachute.

5.

LICENSING – RAISING STANDARD OR RAISING FUNDS?

To compel a man to furnish funds for the propagation of ideas he disbelieves and abhors is sinful and tyrannical." - **Thomas Jefferson**

The Housing Act 2004 brought two major changes for private landlords

- A new definition of a 'HMO'. This meant that properties that were previously considered to be shared houses, were now HMO's provided they were occupied by three or more people, forming two or more households, and sharing at least one basic amenity.

- A means of licensing privately rented properties and the landlord.

Part two of the Act covers licensing of HMO's and part three covers *Selective Licensing* of other residential accommodation.

The Act gave local authorities 3 different types licensing powers.

- *Mandatory Licensing* of HMO's. This covers all HMO's where more than five people, forming two or more households, are sharing one or more basic amenity, on three or more floors. It also applies to properties where a building has been converted into self contained flats, and the building conversion was completed prior to 1st June 1992, or which come under regulation 20 of the Building Regulation 1991, if less than two thirds of the flats are occupied by owners.

- *Additional Licensing* of HMO'S that do not fall in the mandatory class. This allows a local authority to extend HMO licensing to smaller HMO's.

The Act stipulates that a local authority that decides to use *Additional Licensing* "Before making a designation the authority must...

(a) take reasonable steps to consult persons who are likely to be affected by the designation; and

(b) consider any representations made in accordance with the consultation and not withdrawn"

- *Selective Licensing* of any privately rented property in a selected area. Landlords often confuse this with Additional licensing, assuming it only applies to HMO's in the selected area. This is what the Act states:

"(a) it is in an area that is for the time being designated under section 80 as subject to selective licensing, and

"(b) the whole of it is occupied either—

"(i) under a single tenancy or licence that is not an exempt tenancy or licence under subsection (3) or (4), or

"(ii) under two or more tenancies or licenses in respect of different dwellings contained in it, none of which is an exempt tenancy or licence under subsection (3) or (4).

"(3) A tenancy or licence is an exempt tenancy or licence if it is granted by a body which is registered as a social landlord under Part 1 of the Housing Act 1996 (c. 52).

(4) In addition, the appropriate national authority may by order provide for a tenancy or

licence to be an exempt tenancy or licence—

(a) if it falls within any description of tenancy or licence specified in the order; or

(b) in any other circumstances so specified."

Leaving aside the potential cost of bringing a property up to the standards required in order to obtain a licence, there are two areas of concern; the first is the cost of a licence, the second is the potential for a local authority to designate an area for *Selective Licensing*. I have covered elsewhere, the impact licensing could potentially have on a landlords ability to raise a mortgage on a property.

What does a licence cost?

The cost of an HMO licence varies depending on the local authority area. The government did not set a specific fee, or a limit, regarding how much each local authority can charge. One might consider the benefits had they chosen to have a national fee, similar to a drivers licence.

Each local authority calculates the costs associated with implementing HMO licensing - staff costs include training, inspection and administration costs - which include publicity and may all be taken into account.

In theory they are not permitted to use licensing fees for the purpose of raising revenue for other projects, or areas of work, but unless a *Freedom of Information* request is made, their calculations' cannot be challenged; many authorities include the cost of chasing unlicensed landlords in their calculations – but why should law abiding landlords pay for local authorities to do their job?

Some local authorities do support good landlords, and are offering discounts for early applications which included all documents, and full fees, to landlords who are accredited or are members of an association like *The National Landlords Association* (NLA), that can offer support, important information, and assist them in carrying out a more effectual job. Some authorities are recovering monies lost in discounts by increasing the fee to landlords for whom they have to 'trace and chase'. They can do this by increasing the basic fee or by issuing a one year licence, at the full fee, which will attract the full fee again on renewal a year later. This sends a potent message; good landlords will not be made to pay for the bad ones!

Why a licence, under selective licensing, is the same as a HMO licence, is difficult to understand. Many of the properties needing a *Selective Licence* are single occupancy, and are therefore not required to meet so many regulations? Perhaps local authorities could be challenged to show the cost of licensing a single occupancy property?

When the Housing Act 2004 was drawn up, bizarrely they failed to cover the renewal of licences; as a consequence this lead to some authorities charging ridiculous fees of up to £1,000 for a simple renewal. It was not until the time came for licences to be renewed, that this oversight was recognised, and eventually guidance was issued. Most local authorities did not transfer data from original applications onto computer data bases; instead hard copies were retained, meaning landlords were obliged to start from scratch when they applied for a renewal, and this increased the cost. We need to be vigilant in not allowing this to happen next time HMO licenses come up for renewal. Also, we must ensure that that all local authorities comply with the EU Directive which states that all application forms must be available in digital format.

It is the potential for a local authority to decide to introduce *Selective Licensing* that causes most concern to landlords.

Selective Licensing is intended to address the impact of poor quality private landlords and anti-social tenants. It has primarily been developed with the intention of tackling problems in areas of low housing demand, or where there is anti social behaviour caused by the tenants of private landlords.

In an area subject to *Selective Licensing*, all

private landlords must obtain a licence, and this is not just for HMO's. If they fail to do so, or fail to achieve acceptable management standards, the authority can take enforcement action or withdraw the licence.

Before making a decision to designate an area for *Selective Licensing* an authority must consider whether there are alternative means of addressing the issues – for example, through the introduction of a voluntary accreditation scheme for landlords. It must also ensure that any proposed licensing scheme fits with its overall housing strategy, and policies on homelessness and empty dwellings. Despite this some authorities which include Newham, Oxford, and Liverpool, have all introduced blanket *Selective Licensing* of the whole area.

Wednesday, 21 November 2012

"A district council has successfully fought off a High Court challenge brought by landlords over its introduction of a selective licensing scheme in two of its wards.

"The plan to bring in such a scheme for Margate Central and Cliftonville West was agreed by Thanet District Council's Cabinet in January 2011.

"The authority said the purpose of the five-year scheme was to tackle anti-social behaviour and low housing demand, as well as secure

*improvement to the management of privately
rented properties.*

*"The Southern Landlords Association brought
judicial review proceedings, arguing that there
was:*

- *a lack of evidence to conclude that the
  areas were or were likely to become an
  area of low housing demand;*
- *a lack of evidence or basis for determining
  that there was an anti-social behaviour
  problem in the wards which some private
  sector landlords had failed to combat;*
- *a failure properly or at all to consider
  other courses of action to achieve the
  objectives selective licensing was intended
  to achieve.*

*"However, in Southern Landlords Association, R
(on the application of) v Thanet District Council
[2012] EWHC 3187 Mr Justice Cranston has ruled
in the council's favour.*

*"The judge said it was impossible for the claimant
to sustain the contention that there was a public
law error in the council's decision-making.*

*"He said: "The problems of anti-social behaviour in
the Margate Central and Cliftonville West wards
and its causes did not suddenly emerge in 2010....
it has a context stretching back over several
decades.*

""Members of the Cabinet would have been aware of the issues through local knowledge and being informed by the raft of reports about the area over the previous decade. In the light of all that they made a judgment about the benefits of selective licensing."

"Mr Justice Cranston set out the statutory delineation of low housing demand and said it again seemed impossible to him sustain a public law challenge to the council's decision-making in this regard.

"The judge meanwhile said the third ground of challenge went 'nowhere'.

""It is clear from what I have said earlier in the judgment that during the past decade the council has taken a wide range of initiatives to address the problems in the Margate Central and Cliftonville West wards," he said.

""Those were reviewed in the proposal document. It is also clear that, despite those efforts and the public money spent in the area, its regeneration had not been achieved. I cannot see any basis for contending that the requirement to consider other courses of action was not met."

"Mr Justice Cranston concluded that the claimant "failed to establish any error of law in the council's assessment and designation of its Margate Central and Cliftonville West wards as a selective licensing area".

"Thanet, the first local authority in Kent to put in place a selective licensing scheme, described the ruling as 'a significant victory'."

This case illustrates that any local authority can make a case for *Selective Licensing* if there is anything that might be considered anti social behaviour in their area, this might be anything from too many cars parking there, too much rubbish, or criminal activity. Just how licensing a landlord can change any of these things is yet to be seen. Some authorities have used these powers to improve the standards of homes offered by landlords, and has shown to be a sound use of *Selective Licensing*. I am aware of one area where landlords were asked to provide copies of *Gas Safety Certificates,* following the introduction of *Selective Licensing,* in a well defined are. When the certificates were presented, the majority were dated after the request had been made – this provided the authority with demonstrative proof that they had used their powers effectively.

Inappropriate use of *Selective Licensing,* particularly where a local authority designates their whole area, is going to damage the supply of privately rented property in those areas, and could eventually lead to homelessness. Local authorities already have many powers to control the standards of privately rented properties, but the problem is that they are short of resources, and it is only by collecting licence fees from landlords, that they can afford to pay enough staff to perform their statutory functions.

I have covered elsewhere the fact that the lenders are unlikely to lend to an investor who wishes to buy in an area where there is *Selective Licensing;* this is an unintended consequence that local authorities will not be aware of – perhaps this will help us to fight the case against inappropriate *Selective Licensing.*

In areas of severe anti social behavior, landlords are often victims too. No landlord would intentionally accept a bad tenant, and in particular, one with anti social behavior. Unfortunately it is not always easy to stop these tenants until it is too late. Now that local authorities, and RSL, can evict these tenants with greater ease, landlords now face the risk of finding them turn to the private rented sector. We are denied access to information detailing their previous behaviour, and are not informed as to whether these people have already been evicted by a local authority or an RSL. Only by working together and communicating with each other via online forums and at local landlords meetings, can we warn each other about undesirable tenants. Then when we finally manage to evict one, and they are searching for somewhere else to live, any potential future landlord, of such a tenants, has a better chance of avoiding them.

As Paul Routledge, landlord of thirty years, who runs *www.LandlordReferencing.co.uk* (LRS), states:

"Landlords are the gatekeepers of our communities, if we do not let criminal tenants put down roots in our properties they cannot thrive"

Paul started LRS after he almost lost his life as a result of criminal tenants, who brutally attacked him, stabbing him in the head five times, and leaving him for dead. Realising that those tenants would surely move on to another unsuspecting landlord, he felt compelled to find a way of preventing this. LRS is a free service where landlords, and letting agencies, can provide information regarding bad tenants, and where we can all access a lifestyle reference (taken from the information given by previous landlords and agents) and, as mentioned before, a full credit reference.

Local authorities need to work with landlords, and with LRS, as Neighbourhood Watch are. This will send a strong message to bad tenants, 'BEHAVE OR BE HOMELESS'! Only with the threat of homelessness will bad tenants begin to realise that they must pay their rent and treat their community, our properties, and us, with respect. Licensing landlords will never stop the anti social behaviour of some tenants and will reduce the number of affordable homes available to tenants on modest incomes.

MARY LATHAM

6.

UNIVERSAL CREDIT OR UNIVERSAL CRISIS?

"I'm trying to think, don't confuse me with facts." - Plato

If you are considering skipping this chapter remember that every tenant is only a P45 away from needing benefits – will your tenant still be employed next year? If your tenant loses his job and cannot pay the rent will you know what to do? Eviction is a long and expensive process; understanding the benefits system can reduce the burden, and there are significant changes on the way, changes we all need to understand.

'Housing Benefit' became *'Local Housing Allowance'* (LHA) in the Welfare Reform Act 2007 and took affect from 7th April 2008.

'Changes', for tenants renting from private landlords, included the way in which the benefit entitlement was calculated, and the loss of the option to make direct payments to the landlord, for all but vulnerable tenants, or those with eight weeks or more rent arrears. Under LHA, a flat allowance is used to decide the eligible rent of all claimants, with similar sized households, living in a given area, known as the 'broad rental market area', rather than tying the level of benefit to the individual property.

This was supposed to provide an incentive for those on Housing Benefit to seek out cheaper accommodation, and was the beginning of plans to reduce the overall cost of housing to the public purse. One of the most significant changes for landlords, was that a claimant could no longer choose to have the rent paid directly to the landlord. The result of these changes amounted to reduced rents and increased rent arrears; it was the beginning of downward spiral, forcing many of us to refuse housing to those on LHA.

The *Broad Market Rent* (BMR) was calculated by the *Valuation Office* (VOA) and based on evidence gathered from landlords and letting agents; it showed the rents that were being charged in the designated BMR area. The average (median) was used to set the LHA for the number of bedrooms in each BRM area and the figures were published. Unfortunately many landlords failed to provide evidence to the VOA, and in some areas, the LHA was significantly lower than the rent being achieved from non-benefit tenants.

On 22nd June 2010 the LHA system was changed again in an emergency budget and these changes began to reduce LHA rents from April 2011.

The five bedroom LHA rate was removed so that the maximum level of LHA to be paid, would be for a four bedroom property. This meant that landlords who were renting larger properties, with more than four bedrooms, to big families, saw a big drop in their rent.

The following caps were introduced so that LHA rates would not be paid above these rates, regardless of BMA rents. Claims were assessed on the number of bedrooms required rather than the number of bedrooms that were actually in the property.

- £250 for a one bedroom property,
- £290 for a two bedroom property,
- £340 for a three bedroom property,
- £400 for a four bedroom property.

From October 2011 the LHA rates were reduced further, when they began to be calculated at the 30th percentile of rents, in each BMR area, rather than the average (median). Consequently many more landlords were faced with tenants who were not going to be able to claim enough LHA to cover their rents. For those who were housing large families in five, and six, bedroomed properties, there was a vast reduction in the LHA.

On 6th February 2012 I wrote the following article.

The National Landlords Association announced on Friday – *"We have just learned from the Department for Work and Pensions that LHA rates are to be frozen from April this year."*

If you are thinking "Thank goodness my tenants are not on benefits" don't stop reading because one P45 can change all of that. I didn't take tenants on benefits but I now have two tenants on LHA because of unavoidable changes in their circumstances. This means no rent increases for at least another year and that is on top of reductions due to recent changes in LHA.

Anything that forces some rents down will have a knock on effect on all rents, which is why Government are taking this very risky action.

We still have a couple of weeks (until the end of February) to increase the LHA rates, after that there will be nothing that landlords can do. Please complete the simple form from VOA and email it to the address provided.

This is not for landlords who have tenants on the LHA rate, it is for those of us who are getting rents that are above the LHA rate because those rents will increase the average. Once this information is given to the VOA they are legally bound to include it in the calculation for the rate of Local Housing Allowance (LHA). Please ask every landlord you know to do this and, in particular, those who let to students and are achieving a high single room rate. There will be thousands more people on the shared room rate in the coming months because of the rise in the age at which a person becomes entitled to self contained accommodation and the LHA rates are usually well below the level at which landlords can provide good accommodation.

Please do not leave this to someone else, one day you may be very glad that the rates in your area reflect a rent close to that on your AST, but if that rate does not increase before April it will be too late.

We were told that from April 2013, LHA would be calculated as follows:

- 30th percentile of market rents

  or if lower

- current LHAs uprated by the September 2012 Consumer Price Index (CPI)

When the CPI is a negative number or zero, the LHA will be the last determined rate.

The update in April 2014 will follow the same process. [9]

VOA has published the LHA rates that applied from April 2013. The rates were calculated using the lower of the 30th percentile figures from twelve months worth of lettings information, which were collected up to the end of September 2012, and *The Consumer Price Index* (CPI) for September. (The CPI, published on the 16th October 2012, is 2.2%).

These are the rates; perhaps it is worth researching the benefits that your tenants would be likely to receive, should they require assistance?

The LHA rates currently published on LHA-Direct will continue to be effective until 31st March 2013.

New LHA effective from April 2013

BRMA	Room	1 Bed	2 Bed	3 Bed	4 Bed
Ashford	£63.88	£116.74	£138.46	£165.09	£219.23
Aylesbury	£69.27	£121.15	£150.00	£183.46	£288.46
Barnsley	£58.50	£69.23	£86.54	£95.00	£137.31
Barrow-in-Furness	£62.00	£75.00	£91.15	£109.62	£138.46
Basingstoke	£64.90	£132.67	£161.54	£188.68	£253.85
Bath	£71.54	£129.23	£159.20	£183.46	£286.15
Bedford	£63.50	£98.08	£126.92	£153.30	£199.04
Birmingham	£56.21	£96.92	£117.92	£126.92	£165.09
Black Country	£60.00	£86.54	£106.13	£117.92	£150.00
Blackwater Valley	£73.89	£138.46	£173.08	£206.54	£300.00
Bolton and Bury	£45.00	£80.77	£98.08	£114.23	£150.00
Bournemouth	£67.00	£121.15	£150.00	£186.92	£253.85
Bradford & South Dales	£57.69	£80.77	£98.08	£109.62	£121.15
Brighton and Hove	£78.69	£150.00	£188.68	£219.23	£323.08
Bristol	£66.04	£115.38	£144.23	£167.31	£224.05
Bury St Edmunds	£68.50	£100.24	£123.82	£147.40	£219.23
Cambridge	£76.65	£120.00	£137.97	£160.37	£207.69
Canterbury	£73.15	£117.92	£147.40	£176.89	£259.43
Central Greater Manchester	£65.00	£97.09	£114.23	£126.92	£187.50
Central Lancs	£51.10	£87.69	£109.62	£126.92	£160.38
Central London	£126.22	£255.50	£296.38	£347.48	£408.80
Central Norfolk & Norwich	£58.50	£91.15	£114.23	£132.69	£183.46
Chelmsford	£75.08	£121.15	£150.00	£182.78	£230.77
Cheltenham	£66.00	£109.62	£143.87	£170.99	£235.85
Cherwell Valley	£70.00	£116.74	£150.00	£178.85	£229.62
Chesterfield	£48.50	£80.77	£98.08	£112.42	£150.00
Chichester	£70.05	£131.54	£160.38	£196.15	£265.38
Chilterns	£79.72	£138.46	£178.85	£225.00	£357.69
Colchester	£63.50	£102.59	£129.71	£161.54	£200.47
Coventry	£64.39	£91.15	£106.13	£126.92	£167.31
Crawley & Reigate	£78.46	£144.23	£176.89	£218.16	£294.81
Darlington	£56.72	£76.15	£91.15	£105.00	£150.00
Derby	£56.00	£83.08	£103.85	£115.38	£160.38
Doncaster	£53.00	£77.31	£92.31	£103.85	£141.51
Dover-Shepway	£58.50	£86.54	£115.38	£143.87	£176.89
Durham	£65.00	£75.00	£87.69	£98.08	£138.46
East Cheshire	£81.00	£103.85	£129.71	£165.09	£230.77
East Lancs	£53.50	£78.46	£90.00	£103.85	£138.46
East Thames Valley	£74.76	£150.00	£184.62	£226.41	£318.39
Eastbourne	£66.00	£115.38	£150.00	£178.85	£224.05
Eastern Staffordshire	£58.50	£83.08	£103.85	£121.15	£159.20
Exeter	£70.77	£114.23	£138.46	£161.54	£219.23
Fylde Coast	£59.79	£85.15	£114.23	£130.00	£155.77
Gloucester	£64.90	£91.15	£121.15	£144.23	£183.46
Grantham &	£56.21	£74.29	£98.08	£109.62	£150.00

New LHA effective from April 2013

Newark Greater Liverpool	£55.00	£91.15	£109.62	£121.15	£155.77
Grimsby	£53.50	£75.00	£91.98	£97.09	£126.92
Guildford	£83.08	£167.31	£212.26	£271.15	£369.23
Halifax	£64.23	£80.77	£98.08	£115.38	£150.00
Harlow & Stortford	£69.27	£126.92	£161.54	£196.15	£276.92
Harrogate	£67.00	£109.62	£137.31	£160.37	£212.26
Herefordshire	£54.92	£92.31	£117.69	£137.31	£170.99
High Weald	£76.27	£132.69	£173.08	£206.36	£330.19
Hull & East Riding	£56.21	£69.23	£85.38	£103.85	£131.54
Huntingdon	£63.50	£103.85	£126.92	£150.00	£212.26
Inner East London	£94.38	£245.00	£296.38	£347.48	£408.80
Inner North London	£90.45	£255.50	£296.38	£347.48	£408.80
Inner South East London	£88.00	£188.68	£245.28	£305.77	£400.62
Inner South West London	£87.26	£234.67	£294.81	£347.48	£408.80
Inner West London	£102.20	£224.84	£295.00	£347.48	£408.80
Ipswich	£56.77	£88.85	£109.62	£126.92	£170.99
Isle of Wight	£68.50	£92.31	£121.15	£150.00	£187.50
Kendal	£62.50	£95.00	£121.15	£144.23	£178.85
Kernow West	£65.77	£103.85	£129.71	£150.00	£183.46
Kings Lynn	£51.10	£88.85	£110.00	£126.92	£165.09
Kirklees	£55.00	£79.62	£95.00	£114.23	£147.40
Lancaster	£53.14	£91.15	£114.23	£129.71	£138.46
Leeds	£61.50	£98.08	£121.15	£150.00	£196.00
Leicester	£59.00	£88.44	£109.62	£126.92	£160.38
Lincoln	£57.74	£80.77	£99.23	£114.23	£148.27
Lincolnshire Fens	£57.23	£86.54	£108.49	£126.92	£150.00
Lowestoft & Great Yarmouth	£68.50	£85.00	£103.85	£115.38	£147.40
Luton	£57.73	£109.62	£135.61	£161.54	£200.47
Maidstone	£65.00	£121.15	£150.00	£176.89	£230.77
Medway & Swale	£62.50	£108.49	£135.61	£150.00	£200.47
Mendip	£69.04	£92.31	£121.15	£150.00	£176.89
Mid & East Devon	£63.50	£92.31	£123.82	£150.00	£190.38
Mid & West Dorset	£63.50	£103.85	£137.19	£160.38	£196.15
Mid Staffs	£63.50	£90.00	£114.23	£126.92	£167.31
Milton Keynes	£68.58	£115.38	£144.23	£173.08	£219.23
Newbury	£68.12	£121.15	£153.30	£184.62	£253.85
North Cheshire	£53.54	£92.31	£108.49	£126.92	£173.08
North Cornwall & Devon Borders	£63.50	£92.31	£117.69	£137.31	£165.09
North Cumbria	£57.74	£80.77	£96.92	£113.08	£138.46
North Devon	£62.00	£90.58	£115.38	£137.31	£160.38

New LHA effective from April 2013

North Nottingham	£55.60	£69.23	£91.15	£103.85	£138.46
North West Kent	£65.50	£123.46	£150.00	£170.99	£230.77
North West London	£80.81	£176.89	£224.05	£288.46	£346.15
Northampton	£61.32	£98.08	£123.82	£138.46	£183.46
Northants Central	£57.00	£80.77	£103.85	£121.15	£161.54
Northumberland	£65.00	£72.69	£86.54	£103.85	£138.46
Nottingham	£68.00	£90.80	£106.13	£117.92	£159.20
Oldham & Rochdale	£57.73	£83.08	£98.08	£114.23	£150.00
Outer East London	£70.79	£173.08	£212.26	£265.33	£306.60
Outer North East London	£71.54	£153.30	£189.07	£230.77	£306.60
Outer North London	£83.80	£184.62	£236.08	£300.00	£370.00
Outer South East London	£80.23	£153.30	£194.57	£230.77	£306.60
Outer South London	£78.50	£159.20	£200.47	£258.08	£318.39
Outer South West London	£78.50	£206.36	£259.43	£311.54	£392.16
Outer West London	£78.46	£167.31	£212.26	£259.43	£306.60
Oxford	£80.89	£155.77	£188.68	£219.23	£300.00
Peaks & Dales	£68.12	£88.44	£109.62	£126.92	£160.37
Peterborough	£57.50	£91.15	£114.23	£129.71	£165.09
Plymouth	£70.00	£92.31	£121.15	£138.46	£178.85
Portsmouth	£67.96	£115.38	£141.51	£170.99	£235.85
Reading	£75.00	£150.00	£184.62	£211.15	£300.00
Richmond & Hambleton	£67.00	£91.15	£112.03	£126.92	£160.38
Rotherham	£58.50	£80.00	£92.31	£100.38	£144.23
Rugby & East	£61.50	£91.15	£114.23	£132.69	£183.46
Salisbury	£66.50	£117.92	£147.40	£173.08	£229.62
Scarborough	£54.17	£80.50	£103.85	£122.31	£138.46
Scunthorpe	£53.50	£73.85	£92.31	£103.85	£135.61
Sheffield	£61.32	£91.15	£105.00	£115.00	£150.00
Shropshire	£69.23	£86.54	£109.62	£126.92	£167.31
Solihull	£69.05	£114.81	£147.40	£170.99	£235.85
South Cheshire	£53.00	£80.77	£107.24	£126.92	£173.08
South Devon	£63.50	£95.00	£126.92	£150.00	£188.46
South East Herts	£76.41	£139.54	£182.78	£219.23	£288.00
South West Essex	£65.00	£126.92	£158.08	£184.62	£253.85
South West Herts	£78.50	£153.30	£187.50	£235.85	£365.56
Southampton	£64.62	£115.38	£153.30	£182.31	£230.77
Southend	£69.23	£114.23	£149.76	£184.62	£229.62
Southern Greater Manchester	£60.23	£100.24	£126.92	£140.33	£196.15

New LHA effective from April 2013

Southport	£66.00	£89.62	£121.15	£138.46	£173.08
St Helens	£60.00	£80.77	£98.08	£114.23	£150.00
Staffordshire North	£48.10	£79.62	£91.15	£109.62	£144.23
Stevenage & North Herts	£73.50	£121.15	£152.31	£182.78	£229.62
Sunderland	£45.00	£87.69	£100.00	£109.62	£144.23
Sussex East	£66.43	£92.31	£117.92	£160.38	£196.15
Swindon	£65.00	£101.41	£125.00	£150.00	£196.15
Tameside & Glossop	£57.69	£86.54	£103.85	£126.92	£153.30
Taunton & West Somerset	£66.50	£94.34	£121.15	£144.23	£183.46
Teesside	£56.21	£80.55	£96.71	£114.23	£150.00
Thanet	£58.50	£80.77	£114.23	£141.51	£176.89
Tyneside	£60.00	£91.15	£102.12	£114.23	£150.00
Wakefield	£54.27	£86.54	£103.85	£114.23	£150.00
Walton	£80.77	£165.09	£211.08	£271.22	£353.77
Warwickshire South	£66.43	£116.74	£147.40	£173.08	£234.67
West Cheshire	£62.31	£98.08	£121.15	£137.31	£188.68
West Cumbria	£62.00	£79.00	£92.31	£103.85	£135.61
West Pennine	£63.36	£76.65	£85.00	£97.09	£138.23
West Wiltshire	£66.04	£98.08	£123.46	£150.00	£194.57
Weston-S-Mare	£66.96	£98.08	£121.15	£150.00	£184.62
Wigan	£61.32	£80.77	£94.34	£109.62	£150.00
Winchester	£71.58	£145.38	£178.85	£207.69	£306.60
Wirral	£64.90	£86.54	£103.85	£126.00	£141.51
Wolds and Coast	£59.79	£75.00	£92.31	£110.85	£122.31
Worcester North	£58.50	£91.15	£115.38	£126.92	£173.08
Worcester South	£66.94	£98.08	£126.92	£150.00	£184.62
Worthing	£68.08	£117.69	£150.00	£183.46	£241.74
Yeovil	£58.50	£91.15	£121.15	£144.23	£193.85
York	£65.77	£102.59	£121.15	£138.46	£196.15

In the Autumn Statement, the Chancellor announced that in **2014** and **2015**, the uprating of LHA rates will be in line with the 1% increase for the majority of working-age benefits. This means LHA rates for April 2014 will be set at the lower of the 30th percentile of local rents or the April 2013 rate increased by 1%, and the same approach will follow for April 2015.

Very few landlords, who are not letting to tenants on LHA, tend to share their rental figures with the VOA; this has resulted in capped rent levels.

When the interest rates go up and homeowners are forced to pay more for their mortgage each month, they cut their spending in other ways. This is also something the Government are trying to encourage those on benefits to do, but many of them are the fourth generation of a family that has never worked, and whose lifestyle has been structured around the benefits that they receive. 'Cutting their cloth according to the width' is a concept most of these people have not been accustomed to, and many will simply not know 'how' to do it. All men are not created equal and unfortunately some people completely lack the skills necessary in dealing with their own financial affairs.

Universal Credit (UC) is the next big change to the benefit system, it means that all benefits will be paid in one payment. The UC payment will include *Income-based Jobseeker's Allowance, Income-related Employment and Support Allowance, Income Support, Child Tax Credits, Working Tax Credits,* and *Housing Benefit.* The payment will be capped, which means a family can have a maximum payment of £500 a week, and an individual, without dependants, a maximum of £350 a week. 67,000 households will be affected by these caps. Claimants will be expected to manage their own budget, and make this money cover all of their living expenses, including rent. In all but very few cases, rent will not be separated, and can no longer be paid directly to the landlord. This includes local authorities and RSL's who, for the first time, will need to collect their rent directly from the tenant!

When the total benefits in payment before UC amounts to more than the cap, they will be reduced using a prescribed formula. The first benefit to be reduced is Housing Benefit or *Local Housing Allowance* (LHA). This means that a tenant will receive a breakdown on all their benefits and against housing, there may be a reduction below the LHA rate or in some cases no rent at all. There will be some tenants who will refuse to pay their rent because they will be unaware that they have been provided with the funds.

Another very important change, that will cause problems in some households, is the fact that UC will be paid to one member of the household – but which one?

A friend once shared with me, his memories of growing up in the fifties and sixties. He often witnessed his mother weeping on a Friday night, after his father had arrived home drunk, with the news that he had, once again, drunk and gambled away his weekly wages, and there was no 'housekeeping' left for her to buy food for their six children. In those days women with children to look after, were dependant on their husbands to 'give' them money, if their husbands did not provide enough, they resorted to pawning items, or took out loans with official, or unofficial, sources. As we know Pawn Brokers have had a renaissance in recent years, and Loan Sharks are very much 'alive and kicking'. When all of the benefits coming into a household are paid to one person this can take some people back fifty years. Rent arrears have increased enormously since direct payment of LHA to landlords was stopped.

In June 2012 The Guardian Money, carried an article entitled "Rent arrears double in two years"

It went on to report:

"Unemployment and pay cuts force tenants into arrears, while landlords blame implementation of Local Housing Allowance"

National Landlords Association, the leading representative body for private-residential landlords in the UK, have produced a serious press releases, over the years, that tell the story of increasing rent arrears and landlords loss of confidence in LHA tenants.

"New Local Housing Allowance heralds major changes for landlords with tenants on benefit" - 12 Oct 2007

Implementation of the Government's new *Local Housing Allowance* (LHA) for recipients of the existing *Housing Benefit* (HB) will have far-reaching implications for landlords who provide privately rented accommodation, to people on benefit.

Vitally for the landlord, in most cases the LHA will be paid to the tenant, who will take over responsibility for paying rent to the landlord. This represents a significant change from the existing procedure whereby HB can be paid direct to the landlord.

"71% of landlords expecting increase in rental arrears" - 8 Dec 2008

"74% of advice line calls about tenants not paying rent" - 23 Feb 2009

"1 in 3 landlords currently have tenants in arrears" -30 Mar 2009

"A fifth of private-residential landlords have had tenants in rent arrears over the last three months, according to new research published today by the National Landlords Association (NLA).- 16 Aug 2010

"47 per cent of possessions by landlords are due to tenants not paying their rent, according to research published by the National Landlords Association (NLA)." -15 Sep 2010

"Confidence among landlords has dipped for the first time in almost two years, driven by uncertainties including housing benefits and tax changes announced in the emergency budget, according to the latest NLA Landlords' Optimism Index published today.

"Proposed cuts to local housing allowance (LHA) will leave many landlords with reduced rental income and could add to homelessness, according to the National Landlords Association (NLA)". - 23 May 2011

"More than half of landlords have experienced late rent payments in the past year, with housing benefit cuts expected to put further pressure on tenants.

"The survey of nearly 600 landlords found the average late paying tenant owed £730 in late rental payments" - 10 Jun 2011

"A survey by the National Landlords Association (NLA) has found more than half of private residential landlords are planning to reduce the number of properties they let to tenants on housing benefits.

"This response from landlords comes on the eve of the Welfare Reform Bill's report stage in

"The survey questioned landlords about Local Housing Allowance (LHA), with 58 per cent saying they would have to cut the number of properties they let to benefit recipients. In total, 90 per cent of these landlords plan to do so in the next 18 months; with one third stating they would be reducing their LHA properties immediately.

"The survey found that 90 per cent of landlords stated that they cannot afford to reduce their rents to absorb changes to LHA. The large majority of landlords are faced with mortgage repayments and rising running costs." -Sept 2011

"It is clear that tenants favour choice; nine out of ten social housing tenants would like the security of knowing their housing benefit is paid directly to their landlord.- 3 Nov 2011

"A survey by the National Landlords Association (NLA) has found that Government caps on housing benefit payments could force over three quarters of landlords out of the Local Housing Allowance (LHA) market. - 20 Apr 2012

"The survey showed 53% of landlords believe the local housing allowance (LHA) cuts have made it unaffordable to rent to those on benefits.

"Nearly half of landlords (46.9%) believe tenants aged under 35 will be hit hardest by the changes and almost 69% of landlords say they can't see themselves letting to LHA tenants in 2015.

"According to the research, a typical NLA member landlord, with an average portfolio of 12 lettings, has 4 tenants in arrears and the average arrears owed by tenants is £2,363. As might be expected, landlords with larger portfolios have greater amounts owed to them"-June 2012

"Of the 500 landlords surveyed in the NLA's latest Quarterly Landlords Panel, 96 per cent are concerned over problems with the introduction of Universal Credit October 2013

"The evidence shows there is widespread concern about managing Universal Credit online, the implications of it being paid monthly and being paid to one member of a household, and the gap when the current system is phased out and the new one starts.

"There are concerns too that the payment of Universal Credit to one person in a household could, in some instances, upset the family dynamic: potentially putting that individual in a position of considerable power and influence. - December 2012

"Almost eight million adults in the UK do not have internet access according to the Office for

National Statistics, and social housing tenants are estimated to account for half of this demographic.

With the arrival of the digital-by-default **universal credit benefits** *payment just over a year away, housing providers are racing to improve digital inclusion. The new online welfare system will be launched in October 2013 by the Department for Work and Pensions, and 80% of tenants will require internet access to manage their benefits by 2017." [10]*

Stories are now being brought to light, as a result of the pilot schemes, that Government have put in place, to test UC. It is important to note that the *Housing Association* (RSL's) tenants who are taking part in these pilots were chosen because they had a good record of rental payments. The reports present a grim warning.

These are some of the comments made by representatives of those RSL's who are taking part in the pilot scheme taken from Guardian "Top tips: Lessons from the direct payment pilot schemes"

*"**We have four times the level of staffing compared to our normal arrears recovery:** And significant staff resources devoted to communication and making sure everyone understands the changes. One staff member for every 160 tenants."*

"Our project has seen nearly 1,000 tenants

introduced to direct payments, with nearly 180 having their housing benefit 'switched back' for not paying their rent and other charges. Arrears have reached £180,000 since the start of the project – a rise from 2% to 11%. We have also seen much greater intervention with tenants."

"We doubled the number of staff involved in managing the cases on the project"

"Our arrears have increased by £46,000: *As a percentage of the rent collection the figure is only around 2% – but that's the product of a massive injection of recovery work and support, which just isn't scalable."*

"We have tried to get people to pay by direct debit where we can as it is cheaper: *But the reality is you will need to offer a range of payment methods and support. Not everyone will need a jam jar account and most have bank accounts – but are our tenants able to operate bank accounts without causing other financial issues/charges? It is understanding these issues that takes the time."*

As tax payers, I am sure we all agree that people who choose not to work, should not be able to have a more desirable lifestyle, and home, than those who do choose to work; therefore welfare reforms are indeed necessary. Many people have no financial skills, and this is the problem. Even reliable tenants may struggle to manage their money, if it is paid monthly, in arrears, in one payment – this has been the experience of the RSL's. Government is giving local authorities a 'pot of money' called a *Discretionary Fund*. This money is to assist tenants who cannot manage, in particular during the first month, while they are waiting for their first UC payment. These funds are also meant to be used for support services for those tenants, but will there be enough money to do both of these? Will local authorities, who themselves will have to start chasing their rent, use this money to pay rent, or will they 'ring fence' a portion to provide the help and support that so many tenants will need? Will tenants have access to computers, and staff, that can aid them in making their claims online? All UC claims will be made online, as will the tracking of a claim, so there will be no more calling into the *Housing Benefit* department to discuss a claim. On the positive side, claims will no longer be held up, or suspended, because the tenant has failed to produce the relevant documents displaying proof of earnings and other benefits in payment – all of this information will be gathered through a new information sharing protocol, and even employers will be expected to provide information to the system. If tenants are not provided with access to computers, and support, they risk not be paid their UC payment and one can only imagine how that will affect rent arrears. Many landlords will have to be proactive in helping their tenants, and in fact, they will need the tenants password to enable them to track the UC payments online and to know when to expect the rent. If we choose to just 'sit tight' and allow our tenants to struggle, many will not manage their finances, and once they get behind with their rent payments, they may never catch up. The potential for this to increase homelessness is goes without saying, because landlords cannot afford to lose rent in order for Government to reduce the benefits bill.

UC will be rolled out from October 2013 when new claimants will be put onto the new system. From April 2014 existing claims will begin the process of being transferred. By 2017 UC will cover all benefit claimants, this may of course change, since the pilots currently being run, throw up problems. But there is no doubt in my mind that the future of letting to tenants on benefits will mean more involvement with tenants for landlords, because direct payment to landlords will no longer be an option. *Credit Unions* may offer a favourable solution for those tenants who cannot access high street banking facilities, and in particular, 'jam jar' accounts - which help people to budget and enable landlords to provide tenants with a means of placing a standing order on the account to pay their rent. There are several *Credit Unions* that already offer this service, and it is worth ascertaining with your local *Credit Union* as to exactly what services they can provide, and how a landlord can help a tenant go about setting up an account with them.

Many people will need only a little support to guide them through the changes, and they will continue to be good tenants, but there is little doubt that some previously good tenants will not cope. This is going to be a minefield for landlords.

7.

WILL THE HIGH STREET LETTING AGENT SOON BE A THING OF THE PAST?

"Apps and mobile platforms are ideally suited to home-hunting, providing people with the ability to locate properties around them using GPS, make instant calls and emails, and search and research on the move" - Miles Shipside, Director of Rightmove.

Shelter Scotland, the housing and homeless charity, have managed to stop Letting Agents from charging fees to tenants, other than the deposit and first month's rent.

Scottish law was already in place to prevent Letting Agents charging fees to tenants, and Shelter successfully campaigned to get this law enforced earlier this year, thirty years after it had been forgotten. Tenants are now being assisted in reclaiming the fees that they have been charged. Provided these fees where paid during the last six years, they can go back to the Letting Agents and reclaim them. A website, *www.reclaimyourfees.com*, has been set up to assist tenants wishing to undertake this task. .[11]

As can be imagined, Letting Agents are very nervous of the impact this will have on their cash flow; I'm told that some are even closing their doors to prevent tenants making claims against them.

Shelter have now turned their attention to England and Wales, where there is still no legislation in place to prevent Letting Agents charging fees to tenants. Under their "Letting away with it" campaign, they are gathering the necessary evidence to prove that tenants are being exploited by the English and Welsh Letting Agencies. Their research, published on 4th September, found twenty-three per cent of 5,379 adults surveyed claimed they had indeed been 'ripped off' by letting agents. Shelter has stated that it has found cases where renters have been charged £150 every year for credit checks, £100 for viewing a property and up to £540 for administration fees!

The Officer of Fair Trading joined the fray in February 2013 after the report "The Lettings Market" was published.

"The lettings market is a significant part of the UK economy, but it generates a high level of complaints. The OFT has carried out a review of the sector, based on an analysis of a large number of complaints, and considered ways forward to tackle the issues that appear to be problems in the market."

Recommendations in the report include

- Better compliance with the legislation already in existence, and in particular, improved up front information. Ideally we would like fees to be set out in a clear tariff of charges at the start of the process and certainly before any contract is signed.
- Initiatives which make it easier for landlords and tenants to assess quality and compare one agent's services against another, such as recognised logos, which signify minimum standards are met.
- A general redress mechanism so landlords and tenants are able to resolve problems when they occur. This is supported by a number of industry players. Consideration needs to be given to the cost this would impose on traders, and the extent to which it would restrict new entries to the lettings market.
- Mechanisms for protecting money, i.e. more widespread use of client money protection mechanisms and increased

compliance with the mandatory *Tenancy Deposit Protection Schemes.* We believe, in regards to these requirements, greater transparency would be helpful, and any additional steps the UK Government, industry, and consumer groups can take to raise awareness would be particularly useful.

- What more can be done to help landlords and tenants understand and compare what existing codes offer, so they can more easily make informed choices and know what to look for when trying to find a good letting agent?

The report concluded with this undertaking:

"The OFT is keen, so far as its remit allows, to play a role in supporting the development of any overarching strategy. As a next step, in addition to producing this report the OFT will also by the end of this year:

- *Produce and consult on a document which will provide UTCCRs/CPRs/BPRs guidance for letting agents.*
- *Review the substance and accessibility of existing OFT Guidance on unfair terms in tenancy agreements (OFT356).*
- *Work with other organisations to publish 'quick guides' and other information sources for tenants and landlords to help them engage better with the lettings*

process. Sample 'quick guides' for tenants and landlords are published within the report (Annex A).

- *Launch a UTCCRs Hub, similar to our existing Distance Selling Regulations and Sale of Goods Act Hubs, which we hope will be a useful resource for agents and professional landlords"*

The latest assault on Letting Agents fees came from *The Advertising Standards Authority* (ASA) in March 2013. This will have a major impact, enabling tenants to make a choice before even considering viewing a property, in turn this may persuade some Letting Agents to reduce their fees to tenants without further regulation.

"The Advertising Standards Authority (ASA) today ruled against an estate agent for not being upfront about admin fees. We want to make sure that all quoted prices are transparent to ensure that consumers get a fair deal.

"The advertiser did not make clear that administration fees were excluded from the rental price on the property, and an insufficient amount of information was provided for the consumer to establish how further charges would be calculated.

"In future we expect all letting agents to make clear what compulsory fees are charged when letting a property, and they should do this from

the start. For example a property advertised at £1,500 per-calendar-month (pcm) which requires each tenant to pay a £150 administration fee should be advertised as £1,500 pcm + £150 admin fee per tenant.

"Our ruling makes clear that advertisers must include all compulsory fees and charges upfront in the price quoted. If the fee cannot be calculated in advance because of, for example, an individual's circumstances, then the advertisers must make clear that compulsory fees and charges are excluded and provide adequate information for consumers to establish how additional fees are calculated. This means that potential tenants will have all the information they need in the first instance to help them make an informed choice and to avoid being drawn into contracts they haven't budgeted for.

"Our priority now is to make sure our rulings are followed by the sector as a whole. We want to ensure that all quoted prices are transparent so that consumers are not misled or treated unfairly." [12]

Letting Agents, with 'High Street' premises, carry a huge overhead and in order to cover that overhead, and make a profit, it is normal practice to spread the cost of letting a property between the landlord and the tenant. Unfortunately there are some Letting Agents who charge both the landlord and the tenant for the same services, these often include referencing the tenant and or guarantor, drawing up the Tenancy Agreement, taking an initial, and outgoing Inventory. Some Letting Agents charge an Administration fee and do not disclose the services included, which is also giving cause for concern because the additional burden of these costs make it difficult for some tenants to gain access to rented property in the *Private Rented Sector* (PRS). Many also charge on going fees for renewal of Tenancy Agreements, where they could simply allow them to rollover into *Statutory Periodic Tenancies* with no administration required, and therefore, at no cost to the Letting Agent, Tenant or Landlord.

There is little doubt in my mind that Government will be soon be persuaded to control Letting Agents charges to tenants; when this happens many will not be financially viable, unless they increase their charges to landlords, or reduce their overheads.

Labour peer Baroness Hayter, of Kentish Town, is proposing amendments to the current *Enterprise and Regulatory Reform* (ERR) Bill to bring Letting Agents into line with Estate Agents.

"Legislation already requires estate agents to be part of an ombudsman scheme. What this amendment would do is extend that so that letting agents would also have to be members of an ombudsman scheme," she said. *"At the moment*

anybody could set up as a letting agent. They don't have to promise to give minimum standards to the tenants or to the landlords."

The proposal went before the House of Commons on 16 April '13.

My question is *"Do we still need Letting Agents with High Street offices or do most tenants now search for a new home on the internet?"*

I have been letting and managing my own properties for over forty years and I have graduated from advertisements in local newspapers and shop windows, through to using Letting Agents for a let only, advertising on *Gumtree* and, during time I was attracting tenants through these various methods, I was avoiding voids. I stopped using a Letting Agent for the let only after realising that not only was I paying three/four weeks rent, plus VAT – equivalent to an average of £650, but the tenant was also being charged £240! I always use the NLA tenancy agreement. I do my own inventories, and meet and greet all my new tenants. I was lead to believe that my fee was covering advertising, viewings (which rarely exceeded two), and reference checks. I did not expect my new tenants to be charged fees, and this had not been explained to me by the Letting Agent. I used Google to research the alternatives options and consequently discovered *LettingAProperty.com*. Throughout our initial phone call, I found them charming and helpful. My first property was placed with them soon after, and a few days later I managed to let it to a lovely tenant, who is still with me now. The total cost of this amounted to less than eighty pounds. By having my property on all the major websites, It attracted a lot of interest, and I was able to choose those to whom I offered a viewing, saving me time and producing a reputable tenant, who came with excellent references and credit history. I have not looked back since.

All my property details are stored on their system and the individual property profiles can be reactivated whenever I need to find a new tenant. This means I do not have to search for photographs or write a new advertisement, I can however update my photographs and information, should I wish. I activate a property profile as soon as the tenant current living there gives me notice; my advertisement goes live soon after, which means I am not under pressure to accept a tenant who does not meet 100% of my criteria, simply to avoid a void. I choose to fund the referencing of my tenants myself so that my new tenants have only the deposit and first month's rent to find. It is my belief that this sends a clear message to my tenants that I am a fair landlord, who will treat them with respect. I am aware that many landlords are of the mindset that tenants should be charged for this fee, which is perfectly reasonable provided this is explained to the tenants at the outset. How any changes to the regulation of Letting Agents fees will impact on a landlords ability to make charges, remains to be seen.

I am in total control of my business and I feel that I am the best person to decide who will live in my properties. Although I do not require a full management service at this time, if in the future I do, I hope that there will be an online property management service that is as easily accessible as *LettingAProperty.com*. Frankly, I have no desire to pay for the rent and rates of an High Street premises, when those offering these services could just as easily do so from a spare room in their own home, or a simple office tucked away somewhere that does not attract high overheads.

The last revolution, one which made my life so much easier, was the 're-birth' of the mobile phone. Who remembers the days when the answer machine tape was full and hours were spent returning calls, and arranging viewings, only to arrive back home from those viewings, to find yet more enquiries on the answer machine? Then there were the times you would sit at a property, waiting for a prospective tenant who would never arrive, only to return home and find an answer phone message informing y that he could not make it. My Blackberry is sometimes a 'gooseberry', but gives me the freedom to be anywhere, while still managing my properties. *LettingAProperty.com* gives me freedom from admin and overheads, while keeping my properties occupied by good tenants. I am getting closer to the 'unearned income' that the Taxman keeps talking about and I'm saving around £550 on every new let!

8.

LETTING TO STUDENTS IS SEEN AS A SAFE INVESTMENT – BUT IS IT?

"I naively chose a college that was almost as expensive as Stanford, and all of my working-class parents' savings were being spent on my college tuition. After six months, I couldn't see the value in it. So I decided to drop out and trust that it would all work out OK...." - Steve Jobs

"Average UK student debts 'could hit £53,000 in 2013"[13]

Those of us who have children born in the last thirty years were the first to be hit by the changes to further education funding. My eldest daughter, now aged thirty-two, entered university in the second year of the university fees system. The only option for many parents at that time was to help these young people to obtain a Student Loan or to raise the finance ourselves, to fund the further education, to which we had raised our children to aspire. There was no warning of this and many parents, who were themselves risk averse, were devastated by the news because they had not been given the opportunity to plan make financial plans to take account of this additional burden and their children would now be forced to start their lives with a major debt. For some young people this meant that they would not achieve their goals to gain a University Degree. Many of my friends re-mortgaged their homes at a time in their lives where they were looking forward to being mortgage free. Others were not in a position to do this having already increased their borrowings to move up the property ladder. There was a marked drop in university applications at that time and many landlords were left with empty properties for the first time.

By the time my youngest daughter, now aged 29, was ready to go into university the fees had increased further but the dust had settled and many parents had become resigned to the changes in funding and accepted that debt would be a part of their children's lives from the moment they started to earn. University applications evened out and landlords were once again able to rent properties to students.

Before the changes to funding as early as 1999 landlords in some areas had already begun the feel the pinch because the "new universities", that had once been Polytechnics, were going back to being community colleges and attracting local young people who did not need to live away from home. Many landlords turned to other client groups and some sold up. In 2000 *National Asylum Seekers Services* (NASS) was born in order to relieve the pressure on the southern coastal areas where people were entering the UK seeking asylum. NASS contracted with companies who would help them to disperse these people around the country and spread the burden on the local education and health services. These contractors needed landlords to provide the properties in which to house these newcomers, who were often single males, and a whole new market opened up to replace the disappearing students in properties that were very suitable for the new client group. Many landlords signed up to five year, fully repairing, leases and were happy to walk away with a guaranteed rent at student rental levels. A large tranche of property was taken off the market and hid much of the actual affect the changes in University funding had had on the market over the next few years.

In recent years the numbers of students coming from overseas to the UK to study has increased year on year. In 2010-11 66% of those who studied at London School of Economics and

Political Science, came from overseas and in Manchester, which has the largest student population in Europe, 26% of those who studied at University of Manchester were from overseas.

Recent estimates suggest 33,000 UK students are studying abroad, while 370,000 international students are studying in the UK, 102,735 in London alone make up 26% of the total student population in the capital and in my own area, the West Midlands, the proportion is 18% with 36,685 young people entering the region to study at our many highly respected universities. China is the top non-EU sending country and the number of young people from China studying in the UK increased from 56,990 in 2009-10 to 67,325 in 2010-11. The top EU sending country, The Republic of Ireland, increased from 16,595 in 2009-10 to 16,855 in 2010-11

"Growth in China slowed to 7.7 percent in the first quarter of 2013, below forecasts and fuelling fears a recent pick-up in the world's number-two economy is faltering on weak overseas demand."

"The Northern Ireland economy will grow by only 0.5% in 2013 and is still lagging behind the rest of the UK, according to business advisor's PwC."

In 1999 Education Ministers from all over Europe met in Bologna, northern Italy, home of oldest university in the world. At what is known as the Bologna Project it was agreed that they would create the *European Higher Education Area* (EHEA) to promote student mobility throughout the EU to pursue degree courses. Launched in 2010, 47 countries signed up.

This is what El País, the biggest daily newspaper in Spain, reported in 2010.

"The European Higher Education Area was officially launched at the start of 2010, with the aim to harmonise studies across the European space. But in what language? With European universities offering more and more university degree programmes in English, their British counterparts are beginning to worry about losing their market share."

In the Times Higher Education, under the headline "Everyone is talking the talk", warns...

"The increasing use of English in higher education across Europe could cost the UK a vital competitive advantage." So what if English were to become the lingua franca of European universities? "Clearly," responds the UNED president, "the British supply won't cover the current demand for studies in English; the slack is being picked up by the Scandinavian countries

and The Netherlands, for example, which traditionally offer more courses in English.

"There is now a range of courses being taught in English across France to a cosmopolitan array of students drawn to the weather and lifestyle of places such as Grenoble.

"Even Switzerland now takes 23 per cent of its students from overseas, and there are 200 masters courses taught in English.

"Unfortunately, it could hurt the UK. The prospect of polishing one's skills in the international language of business has long given UK universities an advantage. Take that away, and the competition gets fierce - especially when recession looms and a question mark hangs over course standards in the UK.

"At stake is more than just a revenue stream, albeit a vital one. Many countries view overseas students not just as a source of income for their institutions but also as a way to boost intellectual capital because graduates may stay on and work. Talented academics may decide to leave the UK to take up the new opportunities to work and live in Europe."

Another threat to student numbers is people studying for degrees from UK universities without actually coming to the UK. There are several options to facilitate this

Type of provision	Total number of students 2010-11	Total number of students 2009-10
Overseas campus of reporting HEI	12,315	11,410
Distance, flexible or distributed learning	113,060	115,010
Other arrangement including collaborative provision	86,670	74,380
Subtotal - students registered at a UK HEI	**212,045**	**200,800**
Overseas partner organization	291,595	207,805
Other arrangement	155	80
Subtotal - students studying for an award of a UK HEI	**291,745**	**207,885**
Total	**503,795**	**408,685[14]**

In 2006, 9 UK universities had campi outside the UK; in 2011 the number had grown to 25 and 10 more are in the pipeline at the moment.

In August 2012 The Times World Education carried this heading

"Universities Look East, Fueling Branch-Campus Boom"

It went on;

"Newcastle University is one of the latest entrants into the thriving world of international branch campuses, or IBCs. Universities across the globe have now established well over 200 foreign campuses, up from 82 in 2006, according to the U.K.-based Observatory on Borderless Higher Education. Some of these struggling IBCs can be found in the United Arab Emirates, where their overall number dropped from 40 in 2009 to 37 in 2011, but East Asia is fast becoming the world's leading destination for new international campuses. In the same two-year period, Singapore saw a 50% increase to 18 campuses in total and China saw a 70% increase to 17 schools." [15]

"The UK sector's growing involvement in offshore education includes everything from branch campuses and institutional partnerships to validation and franchising." Reported another article in Times Higher Education. It goes on to say *"Some half a million students are studying for a UK degree overseas, the number of branch campuses has nearly doubled in the past four years and other forms of "offshore" education - including overseas partnerships involving joint degrees and niche departments within foreign education hubs - are flowering.... Competition for the pool of international students - whose fees provide an important source of income for UK universities - is increasing globally... Other reasons UK universities can no longer count on*

welcoming ever-increasing numbers of foreign students include a newly tightened visa regime and widespread political pressure to cut net migration. London Metropolitan University lost its licence to sponsor non-EU students at the end of August and is currently engaged in a legal battle to regain it"

Changes to Immigration Rules came into force in December 2012

"The UK Border Agency has announced that a written ministerial statement has been 'laid in Parliament' on 22 November 2012 bringing into Law a number of changes to the Immigration Rules, which will come in to force next month on 13 December 2012.

"Most of the changes are said to be minor amendments to the Immigration Rules, however, the decision to restrict international student graduates from switching into the Tier 1 Entrepreneur visa looks a little more than a "minor" change" [16]

A ministerial statement was laid in the House of Commons on 22 November 2012, by Theresa May, and in the House of Lords, by Lord Taylor of Holbeach, bringing into Law changes to the Immigration Rules, which came into force on 13th December 2012.

These are the changes that relate to students.

"I am also making minor changes to the Tier 4 Immigration Rules on students, including allowing students to start work on a business idea or as a doctor or dentist in training as soon as they have submitted an appropriate application; removing an avenue used by applicants to circumvent our rules that ensure an applicant has sufficient funds to cover their course and maintenance; and extending the period of the interim limit where educational institutions that have not achieved both a satisfactory educational oversight inspection from a specified body and Highly Trusted Sponsor status are subject to an interim limit on the number of international students that can be recruited."

"I am setting the annual allocations of places for participating countries and territories in the Tier 5 (Youth Mobility Scheme)"

But what I find most worrying about the future of the student market, for landlords, has nothing to do with the possibility of numbers of overseas students dropping, while UK students choose to combine travel and cultural experiences with their higher education. It is about something that is a threat to universities all over the world; the world wide web.

Through the use of video and web conferencing, affordable high-speed internet connections and mobile devices, like tablets and smart phones, there now exists a suitable technology to deliver and take part in interactive seminars from anywhere in the world. Imagine University Web employing the top lecturers in any given subject from anywhere in the world. People from different cultures studying and working together, examinations taking place simultaneously within each time zone, marking to one standard, degrees recognised in every corner of the world; all without leaving their own home.

The Society for Human Resource Management (SHRM) is the world's largest association devoted to human resource management, representing more than 250,000 members in over 140 countries. In a survey of 449 randomly selected HR professionals, carried out in 2010 they found

- A majority of HR professionals think that the economic recession has led to an increase in the number of job applicants with online degrees
- Nineteen percent of HR professionals "strongly agree" and 68 percent "agree" online degrees are viewed more favourably today than five years ago.

What surprised me is that, according to RDI, the online distance learning specialists, online studies can be funded with anything from Tesco reward vouchers (I am very serious) to Student Loans. On a lighter note I can't help wondering if a family could now combine online shopping at Tesco with saving for online learning for a Degree – it might sound farfetched, but given the option of my child carrying the burden of a huge debt or buying my shopping and fuel at Tesco from the moment the child is born, there is no decision to make. The other payment options are Flexible payment - Installment plans, Pay monthly, Pay-as-you-go, Pingit and Credit Card payment or Employer sponsorship.

If I were the Chancellor of a respected UK Red Brick University I would want to be the first to offer a combination of on-line learning and cultural visits that include on campus group learning activities. Most universities now have sufficient on-campus accommodation to facilitate visitors for ten to twelve weeks, or to offer exchange programmes with partner universities, and if EHEA is going to work this must be the way forward. Imagine following the same syllabus but spending four of the twelve terms in different countries combining an exploration of the commerce and culture of each. How much more valuable that person would be to an employer and how many more options would be open to that person when entering the world of work? In the present economic climate gaining a competitive edge is vital in kick starting a career.

There comes a time when most parents want to kick our chicks out of the nest; university is a very respectable way of achieving this, but it has not be so very long ago that those who could afford to fund it, sent their children on a tour of Europe. The combined cost of studying at home with short visits overseas would be much less than the cost of studying two hundred miles away and paying rent, bills, and travel.

"For 20 years we've educated our youth into debt when they go to university, but never about debt - that must change" [17]

Some parents have tried to help their children by providing the deposit to buy a property that they can then share with fellow students and which will provide a nest egg to reduce their student debt. As a landlord I did consider doing this myself but I decided that the additional pressure of being the 'landlord' would be detrimental to their experience, and possibly their final achievement. The cost of buying a property in a popular student area is much higher than the cost of buying a property in your home town, where families or couples want to live. The return is proportionally lower but the property can be managed by the parents, or placed with a Letting Agent and would not burden the young person, while at the same time providing a sound investment and potentially becoming a future home. This could of course become a shared home while the young person is studying, which would satisfy the need to kick them out of the nest at much less cost. This is arguably a much more favourable option and one which should be considered by parents who are in a position to fund the project.

On 13th March 2013 it was announced that Thirteen Opal group companies went into administration

"Professional services firm Ernst & Young has been appointed administrator of 13 companies in the Manchester-based Opal group.

"The news follows the appointment of Mazars as administrator of its Ocon Construction subsidiary.

"The companies provide student accommodation and professional lets for 7,200 tenants in Liverpool and Manchester alongside seven other sites in Bradford, Dundee, Huddersfield, Leeds, Leicester, London and Wolverhampton". [18]

Their student block in Birmingham was not mentioned, but this will also close reducing the supply of purpose built accommodation to students, and may help other purpose built providers to fill their rooms, which I know has been a struggle this year.

Since I began writing this in the autumn of 2012 I have spoken to many landlords who let to students, many of whom are struggling to let high end shared student homes for the academic year which begins in 2013. These are the properties that are usually let quickly in late December or early January. Many landlords consider that this will be a temporary 'blip' as it was when fees were first introduced and that the market will recover. Many of the top red brick universities are seeing a reduction in the number of applicants for places for 2013 and I don't think that we are seeing a blip, I think we are seeing the shape of things to come for the student market.

9.

CASH STRAPPED COUNCILS HAVE FOUND A NEW WAY TO RAISE FUNDS FROM HMO PROPERTY INVESTORS AND LANDLORDS?

"To compel a man to furnish funds for the propagation of ideas he disbelieves and abhors is sinful and tyrannical." - *Thomas Jefferson*

At a time when all local authorities are looking at 'creative' ways to increase their income landlords are seen as fair game and the hunting season is in full swing.

Three local authorities have found another piece of legislation to misinterpret. Controlled Waste (England and Wales) Regulations 2012.

Under this regulation, which came into effect on 6th April 2012;

"Waste arising from a domestic property used in the course of a business for the provision of self catering accommodation should be classed as commercial waste"

Leeds, Manchester and Sheffield have decided that some privately rented property should now be reclassified as 'commercial' and are informing the owners that they will be charged if they choose to continue to use the bin collections provided by the local authority. In one case the annual charge for this service will be £13,066.85!! This charge includes a weekly collection of general waste and a fortnightly collection of paper, tins and glass which must be stored in separate bins. These charges include £85 for the 'hire' of each bin, and £19 each for 'admin charges'. The council have calculated the number of bins required based on the number of tenants and are also proposing to charge a 'delivery charge' of £50 per bin for the additional bins that they say are required.

The landlord wrote to the local authority, in reply to their request to pay for the service or find a commercial company which is licenced to their collect waste, pointing out;

"We are private landlords who let domestic properties; the properties are not used in the course of a business, they are occupied by tenants

for residential purposes only.

"Please note that the properties are not subject to service charges, all of the tenants pay for their own services such as utilities and charges such as Council Tax. The waste collection service is already paid for by way of Council Tax."

The local authority replied repeating that the properties had been reclassified under the new legislation and confirming that the collection of waste would stop three days from the date of their letter unless the payment was made.

The landlord contacted *The department for environment food and rural affairs* (DEFRA) and quoted what they were told to this authority.

"DEFRA has clarified the situation and we are not liable for the waste collection charges on two counts.

Firstly the change in wording of the regulations was not intended to change tenanted properties from residential to commercial and therefore there should be no charge for waste collection to properties that are rented under a tenancy agreement and all our apartments are rented under an assured short hold tenancy agreement.

"On the second count we are exempt as we are a small business. We receive small business relief on our business rates"

The landlord included this information provided by DEFRA

"Domestic property used in the course of a business for the provision of self-catering accommodation"

"The 1992 Regulations dealt with "Waste from domestic property or a caravan used in the course of a business for the provision of self-catering holiday accommodation" (Schedule 2, paragraph 6), and classified waste from these premises as household waste for which collection charges could be made.

"The 2012 Regulations carved these premises into separate entries in the table in paragraph 2 of Schedule 1, removed the word 'holiday', and reclassified waste from these premises as commercial waste, which means that collection and disposal charges may be made (except for premises which are covered by the "small business exemption").

"However, the removal of the word 'holiday' was not intended to represent a fundamental widening of the meaning of "self catering accommodation". We did not intend to re-classify waste from properties rented out under tenancies from household to commercial waste. Furthermore, our consultation document did not flag any proposals to change the treatment of properties rented out under tenancy agreements. We remain of the view

that residential properties that are subject to some sort of tenancy agreement are <u>unlikely</u> to constitute 'self catering accommodation'".

The inclusion of the word 'unlikely' gives me cause for concern!

If you are now thinking "phew thank goodness for that". The local authority in this case stopped collecting the waste on the date that they had stated and the landlord is now using a local waste removal company who are charging £5,000 a year. While this is a massive saving on the prices quoted by the local authority it is an additional financial burden on the landlord and the local authority are still being paid, through Council Tax, for a service which they no longer provide.

Article 4 Directions, Mandatory and Selective Licensing and now Waste Removal charges...... where will it all end? At some point investing in property to let, particularly HMO's, is just not going to make sense for private landlords and all the corporate investment that Government are hoping will solve the housing shortage is never going to happen.

10.

LEARNING AND SHARING ONLINE

Prior to the summer of 2011, I was unaware of an online discussion forum, but while surfing the net I came across *PropertyTribes.com*. I was fascinated reading the many discussion topics on the site but what kept me reading was the fact that so many knowledgeable people were answering questions and giving helpful advice, and it was all free. After several weeks I gained enough confidence to post information that I thought would help or at least add to the discussion – soon I was hooked and I am now a regular contributor to this great site.

Later that year there was an announcement on Property Tribes that another free site was being launched but this site would offer landlords a directory of goods and services that we all need, there would also be discussions and articles written by industry experts. When *Property118.co.uk* launched I joined and began reading the excellent articles and before long I was invited to contribute my own articles to the site. All of my articles can be found on the site under my Author profile and I am also a regular contributor to discussions arising from other articles or from questions from landlords.

I forget the first time I came across *LandlordReferencing.co.uk* (LRS), but I am very glad that I did. This site also contains articles, you will not be surprised to know that some of these are mine. Much of the content arises from questions asked by landlords or tenants and knowledgeable people. Many are other landlords who have already dealt with the same issues, willing to offer information, advice and support to let the poster know that they are not alone in their difficulties and that there are solutions. This side of the site is interesting and I reply to questions regularly, but the main purpose of the site is to enable landlords to work together to avoid passing bad tenants to one another and to help good tenants to find good landlords. The site is fully compliant with data protection legislations and landlords can record information about both good and bad tenants and the information is not in the public domain. The reason that landlords pass on information about bad tenants is obvious, but the reason that landlords are passing on information about good tenants is that many of them have a poor credit history and they need to build up good references to give a landlord the confidence to trust them, and this is what the site allows them to do. There is no charge for joining the site and everyone is welcome to contribute. Through LRS Landlords and letting agents can now get both a lifestyle reference and a credit reference (from Experian) for £4.99. In April the site offered us yet another service a No Win No Fee debt collection service. These are some of the most important services we need and they are being offered to us at rates that will not burden us with huge overheads.

When I began searching for a new way to find good tenants without paying a High Street Letting Agents I found *LettingAProperty.com*. This was like striking gold. For £99 and £35 a month I can have my property advertised on Lettingaproperty, Rightmove, Zoopla, Findaproperty, Gumtree, Primelocation, and others, tenant referencing, deposit protected, Inventory template, Tenancy Agreement and rent collection. I don't use all of these services but for those that I do use it's well worth the fee. I speak to real people and real people also speak to those who are giving references and to prospective tenants to match the best tenants to my properties. This service has saved me thousands in letting fees and reduced the chances of a void because my properties are let so quickly, often in less than a week. This is now the only service I use to let my properties and I also write articles for the site to draw landlords attention to their service and to pass on warnings and information to help landlords to avoid the potholes in the road.

I have been a member of *National Landlords Association*, *Landlords.org.uk* the biggest landlords association in the country, for years. I always use their Agreements and Section 21 Notices, which are free to members. When I need help, as we all do at some time, I call the Advice line. I read Landlord Library and UKLandlord magazine to keep up to date with all regulation and legislation and I do not know how I would have continued to manage my properties myself for so long without that support. I get all this for less than £100 a year. I am also very proud to say that I am the West Midlands Regional Representative of the NLA and I really enjoy running landlords meetings, engaging with local authorities, West Midlands Fire and Police and being a part of *Homestamp* (Homestamp.com) which is a unique partnership of all the organisations that are part of the private rented section in the West Midlands. I currently hold the Vice Chair of *Homestamp* and I am very proud of what we have achieved by working in partnership to help to make privately rented properties the first choice for good tenants. To download free guidance document just visit the site.

I am often asked how I find the time to read and write for these sites. A better questions would be what else would I be doing that would give me so much satisfaction and teach me so much? Many of the subjects I have covered in this book were 'born' on these websites and my motivation to right this book came from the realisation that there are thousands of landlords who, like me before 2011, work alone and when we have difficulties we don't know who to talk to. There is really no need when the internet which enables us all to seek help and support. I am now so hooked on these sites that there is rarely a week when I do not visit them, I don't always post on them but reading the discussions keeps me up to date with what is happening in the letting business and gives me early warnings that enables me to avoid some of the pot holes in the road.

In case you are wondering I am not being paid by any of these sites to promote them. I am sharing what I believe to be of benefit to all landlords and letting agents.

I joined Twitter in September 2011 and I chose to follow those people from whom I could learn. Many people see Twitter as a social network site, I see it as a resource to learning and by following those people who share information and headlines of the day I am always up to date with what is happening in the property business. I post as @landlordtweets and I have gained a following of almost five-thousand people because I only post about the property business to help to pass on useful information to other landlords and letting agents. When I open my Twitter account, which I do almost every day, it is like seeing all the newspaper headlines in the world and I choose which stories interest me and follow the links provided.

The world wide web has opened up a valuable learning and sharing resource to all of us but just one word of caution. I see many people giving information with such authority you would imagine that they must be right – this is not always the case and it is very important to check everything you learn before acting on the information given.

SOURCES

[1]www.depositprotection.com/documen...turne d.pdf

[2]www.dailymail.co.uk/news/article-2230036/Landlord-loans-reach-time-high-mortgages-buy-let-deals.html#ixzz2BjFmpTK8

[3]www.penningtons.co.uk/Global/PA%20News/FSA-scaremongering-or-a-whole-slot-of-trouble.aspx?th=CP&pa=27DCA33C-4C64-43A7-A182-89332117894E

[4]www.fsa.gov.uk/pubs/international/crsg_slott ing_criteria_specialised_lending.pdf

[5]www.realestatecapital.co.uk/pdf%20files/REC %2012.11%20ISSUE%20PDF%20LOW%20RES 1.pdf

[6]www.fsa.gov.uk/consumerinformation/produ ct_news/mortgages/lease-options

[7]www.gov.uk/options-for-paying-off-your-debts/fast-track-voluntary-arrangements

[8]www.economist.com/node/21540231

[9]www.legislation.gov.uk/ukpga/2007/5/conte
nts

[10]www.guardian.co.uk/housing-
network/2012/sep/07/live-discussion-digital-
inclusion

[11]scotland.shelter.org.uk/news/may_2012/recl
aim_unlawfully_charged_letting_agent_fees

[12]www.asa.org.uk/News-resources/Media-
Centre/2013/ASA-clamps-down-on-hidden-
letting-agent-fees.aspx

[13]www.bbc.co.uk/news/education-14488312

[14]www.ukcisa.org.uk/about/statistics_he.php#t
able8

[15]world.time.com/2012/08/27/universities-
look-east-fueling-branch-campus-
boom/#ixzz2GCLt4CNB

[16]www.immigrationmatters.co.uk/uk-
immigration-rule-changes-announced-by-
government.html

[17]www.moneysavingexpert.com/students/stud
ent-loans-tuition-fees-changes

[18]www.insidermedia.com

6074154R00081

Printed in Great Britain
by Amazon.co.uk, Ltd.,
Marston Gate.